The Ignorant Majority

Our Reason For National Gridlock

The Ignorant Majority

Our Reason For National Gridlock

by
Len Biser

Petra Publishing Company, Fort Washington, Maryland

The Ignorant Majority

Our Reason For National Gridlock

Len Biser

Published by:

Petra Publishing Company
938 East Swan Creek Road
Fort Washington, MD 20744 U.S.A.

All rights reserved. No part of this book may be reproduced or transmitted in any form or by any means, electronic or mechanical, including photocopying or recording, nor may it be stored in any database or retrieval system without written permission from the author, except for brief quotations in a review.

© 1993 Len Biser. All rights reserved.
Library of Congress Catalog Card No.: 92-85271
ISBN 1-880015-13-7

This publication is designed to provide accurate and authoritative information in regard to the subject matter covered. It is sold with the understanding that the publisher is not engaged in rendering legal, accounting or other professional services. If legal advice or other professional assistance is required, the services of a competent professional person should be sought.

From a Declaration of Principles jointly adopted by a committee of the American Bar Association and a Committee of Publishers and Associations.

10 9 8 7 6 5 4 3 2 1

Cover by Inge Sprock

Printed in the United States of America

Acknowledgment

Special thanks to Woodbury Carter and Richard C. Smith for proofreading the manuscript and offering helpful comments. Any remaining errors in text or thought are totally mine. In addition, I would also like to thank the following persons for their assistance and encouragement: Dale L. Anderson, Terri Burke, Alex and Leslie Norko, Gabriella Pulini, Peter Sprock, and Courtney Williams.

Cover by Inge Sprock

Contents

Chapter 1 - *The State of the Union's People* 11
    Language Champions? 20
    Communication Experts? 21
    Informed and Rational? 27
    Caricature or Portrait? 29
    The Ultimate Challenge 30

Chapter 2 - *Abortion* 33
    History of Abortion in the United States 34
        Roe v. Wade
        Never Say Die
    The Moral High Ground 37
        Absolutely No Abortion
        Absolutely No Abortion Laws
    The Absolute Solution 40

Chapter 3 - *Race Relations* 43
    Affirmative Action 44
    The Effects of Affirmative Action 46
        Affirmative Action and the Black Community
        Affirmative Action and the Country
    The Verdict on Affirmative Action 51
    Justly Into The Future 54

Chapter 4 - *Crime and Violence* 57
    Gun Control and the NRA 58
    Our Judicial System 63
    Capital Punishment—Good or Bad? 67
    Criminal Rehabilitation 67
    Police Brutality 71
    A Sobering Reflection 72

Chapter 5 - *Health Care* 73
    The Malady 73
        We're Number One
        And Sinking Fast
        How it all Happened
    The Causes 81
        Runaway Costs: A Nightmare Come True
        Preventive Medicine: The Costly Neglect
        Dereliction: Waning Sympathy
    The Cure 86
        First A Philosophy
        Then The Proposals
        It's Time To Act

Chapter 6 - *Governing Ourselves* **95**
   A Beautiful Design **95**
   The Times They are Here (Murphy's Arrival) **96**
   Elections Gone Haywire **99**
   The Way Back **101**
      Ban Political Advertising
      Minimize Campaign Contributions
      Debate Pubicly
      Demand Information
      Vote Smart
   The Power Of Individual Action **109**

Chapter 7 - *Education of Another Kind* **111**
   Some Facts on the History of Education **114**
      The Beginnings
      The Long Sleep and Awakening
      Early American Education
      European Influence Takes Hold
      Coming Up To Modern Times
   Where Are We Now? **122**
      Teacher Education
      The Educational Potpourri
   Where Do We Go From Here **131**
      What We Do Not Want
      What We Do Want
      Questions We Must Answer
         1. What Is The Purpose Of Public Education?
         2. How Do People Learn?
         3. Who Should Be Responsible For Education?
         4. How Do We Know If Anyone Is Learning?
         5. What Should Be Learned?
         6. What Kind Of Teachers Should We Have?
         7. What Infrastructure Do We Need?
      Max Rafferty— A Case Study
   A Suggested New Approach **151**
      School Offering Number n
      School Offering Number n+1
      The Real Test
   Epilogue on Education **165**

Bibliography ***171***
Chapter Notes ***173***
Index ***185***

We have met the enemy and he is us!

—Walt Kelley

Chapter 1

The State of the Union's People

These are the times that try common sense. Apt words for Thomas Paine had he been born two hundred years later. No matter, his adopted nation, once spurred to independence and self-government by his little pamphlets, would offer him far fewer readers today. Only TV commercials and videos would be at hand for a mass appeal to common sense, an oxymoron situation in itself. Thomas wouldn't have a chance. Thomas Paine? Who's that? Dunno, probably a new comedian or something.

Since Paine's day, America has been rolling along, our moments both glorious and inglorious, but rolling quite well, that is up until the last twenty years or so. But now it appears we have rolled smack up against a mountain of problems, and each morning we awake the mountain has grown larger and more formidable. We can't seem to dig through it or go around it, and at each day's end our tools seem less and less effective. Looking over our shoulders we see the next generation approaching the mountain even less equipped. Why?

Like soldiers in an army getting stomped in every battle, we look around in total bewilderment. What's wrong? Is it our tactics? The officers? Is it our method of selecting officers?

No, none of the above. The root cause of our ineffectiveness lies elsewhere. Analogous to that army, however, we are too close to recognize it. It's not the tactics, or the officers, or the method of selecting officers. It's not money in politics, or unfair foreign competition, or big government. The problem lies at the core. *We* are the problem, the entire population—every man, woman and child. All of us suffer the same disability: we are profoundly over-entertained and under-educated and this condition alone explains our growing mountain of problems.

In other words, our greatest challenge is not how to make our economy run and democracy function, or how to remove the influence of money from government; neither is it how to bring the races to live together harmoniously, nor how to care for the needy and homeless. It is not even how to prevent the earth's population from destroying its own globe. These are secondary problems, which, every one, are caused by our underlying and ever growing ignorance. Ignorance is our number one problem, and our adversary, and it has found the perfect helpmate in entertainment.

Common sense screams this at us, but we are too anaesthetized to listen; we have ceased taking in real information. Implanted in our psyche are instead convictions. We are great—leaders of the free world, possessors of the most advanced technology, the envy of the world, and so on. How can anyone dare accuse us of ignorance? The evidence, however, is irrefutable and cares little whether we choose to acknowledge it or not.

Exhibit A is our growing list of insoluble problems. In our present condition we are unable to think, discuss, debate, and work our way through any of them. How could we? We have no total picture, no background information, and no practice. We have allowed—no, invited—the media to keep us entertained, not informed.

"You've heard about killer bees, how about killer trees. Scientists have found that trees may be emitting gases contributing to smog ..."[1]

"This is Tom Brokaw. Ford has announced it has driven out of the red ..."[2]

We are content with this trumpery, while listening to our favorite music, peppered with incessant bubbly smile-talk, and occasionally interrupted by one minute of, ahem: THE NEWS.

Today actor so-and-so and actress so-and-so announced they are suing their ex-spouses for .... Actress so-and-so has a birthday today; she's thirty-seven. Last night, a gala affair was held in Hollywood to hand out this months' awards for .... Don't miss tonight's CBS news as Dan Rather, reporting straight from the scene will interview one of the millions starving to death in ....

Rarely do the media compete for our interest with substantive information—there's simply not enough demand to make it worthwhile. We want to be entertained by our news, not informed. The target of the media, therefore, is not our reason but our emotions and fantasies, and it's a target difficult to miss.

Meanwhile, when temporarily removed from entertainment and confronted with commonplace graft and greed, not to mention accelerating deterioration of practically everything, we suddenly get annoyed. Alternately shrugging and griping we finally get mad, shake our fists at those SOBs in Washington, and issue the ultimate threat. "We'll show the bastards, we won't even vote!"

True, most elected representatives have proved themselves ineffectual, but are they the real villains? After all, they're merely a representative sample of us, and do they not give us exactly what we want—form, not substance? Over and over we have driven home the point, this is what we demand. We elect by our emotions. Competence? Rational thinking? Candor? Don't interest us. In fact, we're highly suspicious of candidates too long on ability. We don't trust them; they're not like us. We need someone who speaks our language; smiles celestially, tells us to read his lips, entertains us with jokes, or reassures us with patriotic cliches. Don't bore us with hard information, or expect us to analyze ideas. We don't want to think. We want to believe, to have faith. Thinking is not our "forte". (And we shamelessly mispronounce this word our entire lives.)

No, can't lay all the blame on politicians, or even much of it. Public figures know we won't listen if they tell us hard truths, for sure we won't *vote* for them. We'll vote our fantasies. And we won't even know who they are unless they appear on enough TV commercials or at least one Arsenio Hall show. Every candidate also knows (or discovers immediately) elections are not won by discussing issues; they're won by buying votes, by buying *millions* of them. Votes are bought in the identical way large companies buy into any market, by purchasing TV commercials, slick PR, and media experts. Results guaranteed. All the same advertising techniques apply.

Elections, themselves, are firmly intertwined with our entertainment:

> "We will give the nation family values like the Waltons, not the Simpsons."
> —George Bush, Republican National Convention, 1992

(Taking his boss seriously, Dan Quayle mounted his white horse of morality and rode into the fray, attacking a TV program which featured a woman giving birth out of wedlock.)[3]

Voter reflex, in amounts capable of determining elections, is provoked by pulling the strings of emotion and popular sentiment. Uncover some sex-related tidbits, dig up the hint of patriotic blemish, point out a failure to mention God; these are the proven tactics that get votes, and get them by the *millions*.

Even those seeking out substance during an election receive more enlightenment, or at least as much, on peripheral matters than on the chief issues. The main news invariably focuses on the results of numerous polls, which is the same as reporting which way fickle public opinion is swaying to the latest piquant breeze. Newscasters even report the demise of the entire democratic process without apparently realizing it—describing and discussing more the hyperbole, the commercials, and all other aspects of the circus, than the issues. And even when discussions and interviews *are* held, they are usually less than satisfying. Any lobbyist can speak for at least an hour conveniently disguising, avoiding, and confusing matters until: "Thank you, that's all we have time for tonight."

This is not to say that we are totally bankrupt, with no intellectuals or intellectual aspects to our individual lives. Of course not. Neither can it be said there are none among us with superior skills, knowledge, or ideas. There certainly are. The key word here is *majority*. The number of well-informed, rational-thinking individuals, or the amount of our own inclinations in this direction, are in the *minority*; they are the exceptions not the rule. But, as we love to boast, we happen to live under a democracy, meaning the *majority* rules everything for everybody; *it* determines the present and future for *all* of us. This is not to suggest the majority must be intellectual in order for a democracy to function adequately, but it must at least have the capacity to understand, to process information, and to make reasonable judgements. Without these minimum qualities, the majority cannot rule itself. It is merely so much putty—ready, waiting, and begging for manipulation.

So here we are, some 250 million, pledged to a democracy in which everyone eighteen or over has the same say, but precious few are practiced in arriving at opinions through the hard work of information gathering, discussion, and debate. Practically all of us grew up engrossed in the TV-movie-video world and plodded through a mediocre school system, one which stifled curiosity, discouraged learning, and encouraged excellence only in taking multiple-choice tests. This alone would be enough to render us unfit to govern ourselves, but our adult preoccupation with entertainment has clinched the matter. More and more we have come to depend on the visual image as our means of information—of course accompanied by background music and acted out with practiced elocution--so much so, that when we, the public, need informing on anything it can only be accomplished by way of a TV commercial.

("Wait a minute"—comes the rejoinder—"entertainment has always played a large role in our society, it can't be that bad." This is correct, and even its excesses would present no serious problem [except for individuals] as long as the entire activity did not affect our election process.)

Oh, we all know it takes money to win elections. We even know about the large sums collected for campaigns. But have we ever really questioned whether this tradition still makes sense in today's age of all-influencing commercial television? Do large campaign treasury chests work for or against democracy, for or against the interest of the majority? Is there really a good argument for the practice of collecting campaign contributions? Or do we simply assume all voluntary contributions are inherently good, an inseparable part of the process, the American way?

After the public fury over Watergate, we saw, in fact, campaign laws passed to limit donations to national candidates at $20,000 for individuals, and prohibit them from corporations and labor unions. Today we see these laws openly circumvented, and yet make no audible complaint. "Soft money", declared for the purpose of "administrative costs" or "party-building activities", is allowed to pour through these convenient loop-holes to the tune of millions and

Chapter 1 - The State of the Union's People

millions of dollars.[4] George Bush nominates ten of the mega-donors ($100,000 or more) for ambassadorships and eight are approved by the Senate. Large corporations, such as U.S. Tobacco Company, Phillip Morris, and Merrill Lynch, as well as special-interest groups, such as the National Education Association and American Federation of Teachers, are suspiciously high on the list of mega-donors.[5] Solely by spending money these groups are able to defy the needs of us, the majority, while pushing their own agendas to the forefront.

All of this takes place openly. Observe Benjamin Ginsberg, chief counsel for the Republican National Committee, together with a spokesman for Archer Daniels Midland, both *explaining* these contributions as idealistic support for the principles of the democratic process—*to increase the numbers of those who vote.*[6] Is this credible? Do you believe it? Does anyone believe for one moment that these organizations, in the throes of their competitive existences, would spend these sums for the altruistic motive of increasing the numbers voting? Do we enjoy being taken for naive asses?

In truth, as everyone should know by now, campaign funds are *the most important element* in our elections. The chief use of political campaign contributions is to purchase TV commercials, and TV commercials deliver more votes than any other means available. They indeed determine the votes of millions, inciting them to vote in reaction to some carefully contrived, often blatantly false, and completely staged, mini-melodrama, having nothing at all do with the democratic process. In fact, it has replaced it.

Meanwhile we continue to voice, as well as follow, the cliche "get out and vote", the unquestioned assumption being that increased numbers voting is always good for democracy. Nonsense. Which is better for a democracy: to have elections determined by those caring enough to inform themselves—those following the issues and the proclamations and arguments of the candidates—or by millions whose votes are harvested by fifteen- or thirty-second appeals to their emotions, especially their fears? What do we expect from the latter other than guaranteed victory to the biggest spenders? The campaign money solicitors and providers know this. What's wrong with the rest of us?

Should we not first and foremost encourage the self-informing process, and let the natural process of voting follow? What is admirable about millions and millions voting the latest vacillation of their mood? Is this the democracy we're so proud of? Can we ever hope to resolve anything but popularity contests with such an ideal?

Granted, the original idea behind the push for voting was to overcome public apathy. It was automatically *assumed* voters would inform themselves, at least to some degree. At best, this was always a dubious assumption, but in today's world of television, it's totally erroneous. Greater numbers voting is not what we need; we need thinking, educated voters, *regardless of the number*. Only these participants can be beneficial to the process and therefore are to be encouraged. Let the uninformed stay out of this. After all, by choosing to be uninformed they have decided for the ride only, and the ride is all they should get. Why hand them the steering wheel?

It is, of course, no longer news that we are a poorly educated country by modern standards. Not so clear, apparently, is the seriousness of our present state of entertainment-wealth and education-poverty. What's more, our condition prevents us from even recognizing our ailment much less beginning the process of cure. This dismal state of affairs is expressly tragic and unfair towards every child newly born into this country. Not only are we manufacturing a mess for ourselves, we are ensuring in our mischief that the coming generation will be even less-equipped to deal with it when we leave.

Our public-education system is miserably ineffective—in the vernacular—it stinks! We even have the uneducated teaching the uneducated, and horror stories of such magnitude and frequency that we no longer even flinch. Surveys and studies have revealed such truths as: "only half of California adults could identify Japan on a map",[7] 50 percent of managers are unable to write paragraphs free

Chapter 1 - The State of the Union's People 19

of grammatical errors, and in 1989, out of 24,000 international students,[8] age thirteen, Americans scored last in mathematics and were among the worst in science. These of course are only samples. Bungled public education is ruining us, and yet the "educational institution" bands together to fight off real reform, seeing it as a threat to their existence. (Note the large political contributions of the NEA and AFT mentioned previously.) Like a drowning person they will grab at anything. Most convenient is the automatic charge that reform will be unfair to the urban poor. Never mind the plight of the nation.

Educators, however, are only part of the total problem, no worse than the rest of us, just in position to do more damage. Collectively, we, the majority, are one big insanely unaware family, promenading hand in hand, heads engulfed in a fluffy cloud of entertainment, merrily on our way towards the precipice of ruin.

* * *

Let us together either prove or disprove these harsh opening statements. Let's examine some of the chief challenges facing us today and observe our ability or inability to meet them, looking first at the issue of abortion, which keeps us in constant turmoil, and then race relations, which we cowardly continue to circle around. Crime and violence, our claim to infamy, celebrated in our entertainment and more senseless in its enactment than anywhere else in the world, is, by itself, a litmus test. As an example of our easy vulnerability to propaganda and manipulation, we will open up the issue of Health Care, and to demonstrate one clear-cut direct accomplishment of our voting majority we will look into the state of our political process. Finally, we will arrive at the area of most damage, the one in which the only hope for our future resides and which, appropriately, should be declared a national disaster—our educational system.

While examining these issues we will also attempt to apply some common sense toward solutions. But before beginning let's take an honest glance at ourselves—who and what we are. Let's examine some of our general characteristics, just to be certain we are discussing the same people.

Language Champions?

No one would contend we are a particularly articulate people, placing much value in language and its mastery. The fact is, however, we are not even language competent. Not when most of us heedlessly butcher it everyday, viewing its correct usage by anyone else as pomposity or some sort of nerd trait. Not when virtually the *entire* nation is unable to conjugate the infinitive "to be" to agree with the number of its noun, when it happens to be preceded by those impish words "there" or "where". That goes for Carl Sagan,[9] Sen. Pat Schroeder ("There's two reasons ...")[10], George Mitchell ("There's two pieces ...")[11], Les Aspin ("There is aspects ...")[12], Leon Panetta "There's three ...")[13], Sen. Jack Kemp ("There's two ways ...")[14], and of course George Bush ("There's lots of reasons ...")[15] — virtually every one of our public speakers. To all it's simply: "Where's my book, I mean where's my two books? Okay, where's those two thousand books I ordered? Well, there's lots of books here anyway so surely you could loan me one."

No one even notices, much less cares. And what ever became of the verb *lend*? Its permanent banishment presages the fate of more parts of the language. Certainly "there are" and "where are", are on their hurried way to extinction.

Even the college educated among us can be regularly heard to say "idear", "anyways", "irregardless", "warsh", "ruf" (roof), "winda" (window), and so on. (Not to mention our elite in "gov'ment".) Obviously, elimination of such elementary mistakes is no longer considered an essential part of a college education.

In defense of our colleges, a large part of our language disability can be attributed to daily media slaughter—their steady stream of solecisms subverting what little competence remains. For example, in a recent movie titled *Roxanne* the holder of a doctorate in astronomy is portrayed as saying "two pairs of stars revolving around each other ..." when she obviously meant only two stars, that is, *a pair* of stars. Admittedly this could also have been an intentionally accurate portrayal of the astronomer. In either case the point is the same.

This maligning of the language by those at the top of our educational ladder tells us enough. There's no need to broach the everyday language, with which the majority of us attempt to communicate. It's colorful, true, but ineffectual. It's totally awesome and, like, really cool and all that, but in terms of communicating, well, you know, it's just not quite up to snuff, if you get my drift. Do you see what I'm sayin?

Unfortunately, we can no longer afford to laugh at this. Self-government can only work if those voting, first are informed, and second, can think and debate. Language is our chief tool, and we can hardly be optimistic about solving anything if our tools become blunter and blunter.

Communication Experts?

We like to, but we can't correctly claim this characteristic either. Of course, it is possible even with defective language to communicate effectually, merely by first organizing one's thoughts and then expressing them in coherent packages, such as complete sentences and paragraphs. Unfortunately, this ability also eludes us. Not even our professional spokes-persons are adept at it.

But let's begin the examination of our communication skills by looking again at those coming out of our highest institutes of learning. Listen around. You will not hear complete sentences. You will not hear distinctions, much less nuances or subtleties, conveyed by carefully chosen words. Instead you will observe communication via standard crutches. To such teenage favorites as: "like", "you know", "you guys", "dude", "neat", and "gross"; college graduates have added, among others: "in terms of", "with regards to", and "this point in time". We're talking big time crutches here.

Communication does occur of course. Colloquial expressions are effective for conveying a sense of belonging, of being "in". They are also adequate for the standard expressions of disgust, pleasure, surprise, and so on. But, we must admit, they fall far short of communicating precisely, concisely, and clearly. Glaring grammatical errors, celebrated in country music, may be absent from the speech of college graduates, but that doesn't save listeners from still being led on wild-goose chases by vague expressions and ill-chosen words.

Some of the worst examples flow from the lips of our most distinguished personalities, notably a few of our recent presidents. When ad-libbing, we have seen them stop, suddenly remember something else, and then spring to another phrase to complete their remarks. One realizes afterwards that the initial words were merely filling time, waiting for something better to come along. Presidents are not alone. Politicians; entertainers; business people; scientific and medical professionals; spokes-persons for associations and unions; radio and television newscasters and personalities; all provide daily examples of poor communicating.

The Great Communicator

The epitome of our perception of communication is ex-president Ronald Reagan. Elected by the overwhelming majority of us, not only once but twice, he was heralded as the great communicator. In one sense he was; he could communicate unreality. He could tell a story. He made us feel good. He told us what we wanted to hear and employed means we could relate to: anecdotes, jokes, and a large dose of heroic, patriotic talk. Ronald Reagan had "the rarest kind of ability to evoke the spirit of America."[16] That was understandable. Ronald Reagan was the first actor to become president. He could not have been better trained to lead a nation hopelessly brainwashed by entertainment. After all, unreality—television, movies, acting—is exactly what we do understand. We absorb it five or six hours daily. It moves us, stirs us, touches our very souls. Obviously real communication, or communication of reality, never took place. Despite the extreme laxity by the press and other media in reporting critically, it was common knowledge that Ronald Reagan showed little interest in any but a few passionate interests and was unable to articulate and formulate problems precisely. In one meeting, packed full of high ranking officials and congressmen, which we can assume was typical because of the attitude it reveals, Reagan's only contribution throughout an entire one and a half hours was to interrupt to tell about a movie he'd watched the night before —*WarGames*—and then proceed to tell everyone the plot.[17]

Time after time he demonstrated only a single-talent ability to follow a script; as soon as he departed from it, he immediately exposed his incompetence.

> "We would not deploy ... until we sit down with the other nations of the world, and those that have nuclear arsenals, and see if we cannot come to an agreement on which there will be deployment only if there is elimination of nuclear weapons."
> —President Ronald Reagan, 31 October 1985

He was clearly incapable of being anything but a fictional president. No matter. We loved him for the illusion.

Reagan exited the stage after eight years, savoring his best acting performance ever. We were, and still are, left with the aftermath, the reality that somehow won't align itself into a happy ending. Most likely, he has never felt a tinge of guilt; he gave us exactly the performance we wanted.

During those eight years, however, we witnessed corruption and mismanagement on a scale not seen since the Teapot Dome scandals of the Harding Administration. We followed Reagan's Attorney General, Ed Meese III, through continuous investigations, and witnessed his Nuclear Regulatory Commission director, Thomas M. Roberts, taking the fifth Amendment. There was, of course, the bazaar Environmental Protection Agency Superfund scandal and the flagrant activities of aides Lyn Nofziger and Michael Deaver, indicted and convicted of various transgressions in the race to enrich themselves.

Influence peddling was everywhere, challenging us to do something about it. Dozens of former officials earned millions in consulting fees for their efforts in obtaining HUD housing subsidies and grants, the most prominent among them being the infamous James G. Watt, Reagan's Interior secretary. For making a few telephone calls that resulted in HUD backing for three projects, he admitted receiving $420,000, although he could not claim the slightest expertise in housing.[18]

We saw the Pentagon rocked with scandals, ranging from the Small and Disadvantaged Business program up to the largest defense contractors. The Wedtech scandal alone entwined Lyn Nofziger, SBA Administrator James Sanders, Meese, Meese's top deputy James Jenkins, and Meese's friend E. Bob Wallach. Already at the beginning of Reagan's second term there were 131 separate investigations pending against 45 of the Defense Department's largest contractors.[19]

In addition to the Pentagon, HUD, EPA, NRC, and SBA we witnessed abuse of their positions by Reagan appointees in a wide range of federal agencies, departments, bureaus, and commissions, such as the:

Postal Service
Federal Aviation Administration
Agriculture Department
Health and Human Services Department
Federal Home Loan Bank Board
Veterans Administration
Federal Emergency Management Agency
Legal Services Corporation
U.S. Commission on Civil Rights
Transportation Department
Consumer Product Safety Commission

Economic Development Administration
Social Security Administration
Bureau of Land Management
Occupational Safety and Health Administration

By the end of his term we knew of a total of 138 officials in his administration either convicted, indicted, or under investigation—an all-time record.

Worse than these scandals, though, we suffered more direct hits and damage from Reagan's irresponsible form of deregulation. The gates flew open for Ivan Boesky, Michael Milken, and their followers, to become billionaires at the expense of thousands of companies, who were either gobbled up and plundered or greenmailed out of large pay-offs. We watched the frenzy of leveraged buy-outs and merge and acquisitions drive up the national debt and occupy the attention of corporate leaders more than their own business operations.

The intentional weakening of the Security and Exchange Commission, gave a green light to insider trading on Wall Street and illegal dual trading (trading for themselves just before placing large orders for customers) by futures traders in Chicago. One man, Dennis Levine, used his advance knowledge to rake in $12.6 million.

We watched in horror on Monday, 19 October 1987, as the stock market came crashing down to a near total collapse, saved only in the last moment by the Federal Reserve Board and a rally of the Major Market Index on the Chicago board. Ronald Reagan, of course, had no idea what was happening, as evidenced by his Wednesday comments to the press, that the markets had experienced "some kind of a correction."[20]

Next came the Iran-Contra scandal, and as it unfolded before our eyes we did what we do best—we disregarded the tough questions of illegality, of public deceit, and of presidential disregard for democratic rule, and opted instead for entertainment. Millions of us used the TV hearings as a soap opera, tuning in on Oliver North's dramatics and tuning out the hard facts. We watched Ollie play his patriotism to the hilt, eyes glistening with emotion, and we developed "Olliemania" to the point of threatening the Chief Investigator Arthur Liman.

We were then treated to Ronald Reagan's performance in the art of sincere lying, which surely would have won for him an academy award nomination had he still been in Hollywood: "We did not—repeat—did not trade weapons or anything else for hostages nor will we."[21]

Completely missed by us was the reality of what we were staring into—a complete breakdown in our 200-year-old form of government. The executive was lying to and deceiving the legislative and the population—breaking the law more seriously than Watergate and covering up in the same manner. Ronald Reagan, thanks to our uncritical admiration, had taken it upon himself to change our system to a monarchy. He, of all people, he who knew dangerously little of anything,[22] had decided to wage his own secret foreign policy behind everyone's back. His deceit has to be judged much more serious and potentially damaging to our democracy than Nixon's Watergate. Still, to this day, we are reluctant to criticize him.

Notwithstanding all this, there was one Ronald Reagan catastrophe that overshadowed all others and promises to do damage for another generation to come. And he was not the only one asleep during its occurrence. Together with executive branch regulators and congressional overseers of the financial institutions, the press also looked the other way, as deregulation of the Savings and Loan Industry set loose an army of irresponsible managers and downright criminals. As a consequence, the S&L fiasco became our worst financial scandal in history, raising immensely our already dangerously enormous deficit. The bail-out cost estimate quickly doubled and trebled, reaching a trillion dollars in 1990. Thanks to Mr. Reagan and his equally amateurish and opportunist associates, we will pay for this bail-out for the next thirty-three years!

In spite of this plethora of disasters, what impressed us most was Ronald Reagan's firing of the air traffic controllers, his quipping performance following an assassination attempt by a movie-lunatic, and his military action in tiny Grenada. These actions communicated to us. This was more like Hollywood; this we understood.

The story of Ronald Reagan evinces beyond all doubt our inability to receive communication of anything other than emotions —fears, hopes, and fantasies. Facts and real information have almost no chance of getting through, much less processed. In the meantime reality proceeds—steadily destroying us.

Informed and Rational?

If we concede we are no language enthusiasts and aren't particularly good at communicating, then we can't be left with much faith in our ability to stay informed and responsibly debate complex matters. In fact, the more we talk—the more journalistic reports, discussions amongst "experts", and interviews with the man on the street we have, the more confused the issues become. Take, for example, interview responses from public officials. Most often they could be characterized as merely rambling for an appropriate amount of time, thereby forcing the interviewer to move on to the next question. No one complains, probably few even notice, so fixed are we on impressions rather than substance.

Public officials are not totally to blame either. For in the current atmosphere, the reporting media, rather than focussing on substance, lie more in wait for a nugget to drop, which they can then turn into something *sensational*. The situation is further exacerbated by short-cut reporting, concentration on the theme-of-the-week, and the general use of show and glibness in place of boring depth and accuracy. In Ronald Reagan's tenure the press even fell into the passive role of simply accepting and passing on White House briefs. Jeff Gralnick, executive producer in 1983 of ABC's World News Tonight is quoted in Mark Hertsgaard's book *On Bended Knee*: "It's my job to take the news as they [the administration] choose to give it to us and then, in the amount of time that's available, put it into the context of the day or that particular story."[23]

The question is which will come first, news media responsibility or public demand for it. Judging from Gralnick's remarks, it won't be the news media which move first.

To get even more of a flavor of how ill-prepared we are to analyze and debate, examine the airing of these two reports over National Public Radio.

> Studies show 12 percent of the population is black, but 44 percent of the prison population is black. Conclusion: blacks are being discriminated against in the justice system.[24]

This leap to a simple conclusion is typical. No effort is made to look into, and discuss honestly, the facts behind these statistics. That would require reasoning and thinking on the part of the audience, and wouldn't lend itself to a glib journalistic fifteen-second snippet. In fact, blacks commit more crimes (a survey of victims demonstrated this). "Why do they?" should be the next question. This leads one to poorer neighborhoods and less hope of a job. Why is this? Little or no education. Why is this? And here we come to many reasons. Seriously concerned individuals would look into each of them.

> A study is reported as showing 34 percent of blacks being refused home mortgages compared to 11 percent Hispanics refused and something like 12 percent whites refused. The automatic conclusion of the commentator: blacks are being discriminated against in mortgage lending.[25]

Why automatically this conclusion? Do money lending institutions logically turn down loans because of the race of the individual or because of the risk to their money? This leap to the conclusion of racial discrimination indicates more an interest in trumpeting a particular cause than in providing information for thought and debate.

Caricature or Portrait?

So far we've discussed what we are not; let's look at what we are. A useful device is to imagine ourselves as seen through the eyes of a first-time visitor to the U.S. To get to know us quickly our friend would be inclined to sit down in the living room and attempt conversation with us face to face, notwithstanding the TV set blaring away in competition. Of course, he'd stand a better chance accompanying us to the video rental store—where we spend over six billion dollars annually. On the way some conversation could be shouted over the blaring radio, but it would most likely center on the recent movies or videos we've seen, some as often as three or four times.

Looking around him our observant visitor would be struck by our religious ostentation, seeing it everywhere worn on our sleeves, or at least pasted to our car bumpers. He would notice religious convictions freely substituted for facts, and in some matters, such as education and abortion, would find them the sole consideration. No doubt he would shake his head in utter disbelief upon witnessing TV evangelists, of varying degrees of acting ability, command the attention of millions, and gasp for air when told of the millions of dollars that pour forth from viewers into their coffers.

He would, of course, hear of the legendary durability of the famous Jimmys, Bakker and Swaggert, who were able to pull it off even in the immediate aftermath of irrefutable exposure. And no doubt he would utter an embarrassed laugh as, on the TV screen, he watched elderly ladies and gentlemen (as well as younger ones), charged with emotion, absorbing the charlatanry with unbelievable gullibility, faces aglow like children at a circus.

He would be unable to suppress outright hilarious laughter when told of the famous feat of Oral Roberts, of his success in raising millions of dollars by revealing to his credulous audience of millions that God had broken his long silence and, out of the five billion souls on earth, had spoken to *him*, Oral Roberts, threatening to take him away from this life if he didn't raise enough money for the church.

Our visitor might feel an urge to explain to his American hosts that religion is a deeply personal matter, a mighty struggle to know if there's an after life, and that for many the search has not yet ended. He might even point out that it is courting disaster for a society to base its laws solely on the morality and convictions of any religious holding. To illustrate his point he could cite the disaster of *prohibition* in the U.S., as well as the deadly ruthlessness of contemporaneous religion-based governments.

Accompanying us to the mall or eavesdropping on a couple who have just met, our visitor would marvel at what aficionados we are of entertainment. Looking around at the mall, he would be struck by the profusion of entertainment offers—records, videos, video games, arcade games, even baseball-card shops. Tuning into the couple's introductory conversation, as they struggle for common ground, he would hear them discussing their favorite movies, actors, actresses and singers, and nothing else. Walking into one of the two or three book stores he would again be confronted with these entertainers, his eyes assaulted by biographies, autobiographies, and an amazing number of books authored by these versatile heroes— America's rich and famous—almost all of whom got that way by entertaining us in some way.

Having heard in his own country about the writings of Neil Postman, describing the process of Americans *Amusing Ourselves To Death*, he would no doubt attempt to get a copy in the original text. But, upon asking, would meet only with puzzled looks, finding it nowhere, except in the library.

Our visitor would go away with a portrait of us as surprisingly unsophisticated for a modern-day people. No doubt he would also reflect that we were once leaders of the world and wonder what had happened.

The Ultimate Challenge

We've now had a quick, harsh look at ourselves—interests narrowing, attention spans shrinking. The few still struggling to address serious issues, struggle alone, as evidenced by Sen. Rudman's lone effort to address our enormous deficit, while his colleagues steadfastly continued to place political endurance ahead of all other considerations, including survival of the economy.

How do we stop this incessant march towards mindless self-destruction? Can anybody save us from ourselves? It's doubtful. It seems inevitable that mankind, once attaining his basic needs, is doomed to indulge in more and more entertainment, allowing everything else to deteriorate. Historians constantly discover new ruins of past civilizations as well as the causes of their ruin. Other than natural catastrophe, the chief cause is always human foolishness. Usually it's the act of ignoring the limitation of resources and depleting them anyway, with no thought for the future.

We are far along in the process. Most of us don't concern ourselves with major issues or problems, not until they directly affect us. We can't offer much help in solving them, anyway. Aside from being ill-informed, our educational system has left us without the necessary confidence in ourselves. Consequently, we are content to leave everything to slick talkers, content to be told that problems are not really there or that more study is needed. Strangely, though, many of us continue to vote, relying on our gut feelings, of course. It makes us at least *feel* like we're doing something.

Others among us grab the opportunities to cash in on this bonanza of ignorance. Some businesses thrive on it, TV evangelists of course, but many others have established thriving enterprises based on our woeful lack of knowledge. Some are illegal, but the fear of getting caught is no deterrent, not if there's enough money in it to buy lawyers. Under our proudly advertised system, if lawyers can't get you off on some technicality, at least they'll string things out forever.

Hopeless? Could be—except for one glimmer yet to be fully extinguished. Required, however, is a revolution in our approach to education, and decades of time, time for a future generation of healthy, confident minds to emerge. And the first step is to cease hindering our children's education by inflicting them with our own limited and skewed knowledge. Simply by tapping into their natural curiosity, allowing them to develop as thinking, confident individuals, we would be unleashing our greatest power. It remains to be seen if enough of us will awake to and embrace this truth, and then act accordingly.

Perhaps we can also take heart in the words of Marshall McLuhan and Quentin Fiore:

> "There is absolutely no inevitability as long as there is a willingness to contemplate what is happening." [26]

Perhaps.

It's time now to examine six of our major problems. There are of course many more, but these will serve our purpose—to see ourselves and our approach to problems in proper perspective. The remaining chapters will attempt to lay out each problem, including its history, examining how we have thus far dealt with the issue or failed to, and discuss suggestions for solutions.

It's a challenge we owe to ourselves to meet, if we truly appreciate our good fortune as a nation. We owe it even more to those who have gone before us and left us with more, not less, prosperity. Most of all, we owe it to those whose day is yet to come. To fail to meet the challenge will be an act of cowardice and apathetic negligence, sufficient to wipe out forever all the good previously produced in our nation's short history.

Chapter 2

Abortion

Religious freedom hasn't quite arrived in the U.S. Of course, any one of us is free to declare his or her belief in Jesus, or profess to be "reborn", without suffering intolerance or denunciation. But the same cannot be said for non-Christians, at least not if they require public approval. A candidate for public office, for example, daring to admit to religious doubt is finished before he starts. Anyone in the public school system admitting to the same heresy is immediately backed up against the wall by angry, Bible-wielding mobs. We, the American people, flatly refuse to believe that human beings not professing the Christian faith are fully human—capable of the highest human feelings and actions. Never mind the numerous Christians or professed Christians who obviously come up short in these qualities; we forgive them, not so the heretics.

This unacknowledged, unspoken religious intolerance not only undermines the health of many of our institutions, it inhibits free exchange of ideas. On the issue of abortion, for example, it has been absolutely deadly, totally obstructing rational discussion. In this atmosphere, even the good minds entering the dark caverns of dispute, and doing their best to cast light on the subject, have no effect. Only a minuscule number read what they have to say. The rest of us are out there slugging it out at gut level, unencumbered by the weight of factual information. The conclusions, however, of these little-read deliberations point out what common sense already knew—the best solution is a reasonable compromise. But compromise on emotionally-charged matters is not in our make-up. No sir! We've been toilet-trained to believe in absolutes, and fight for or against them to the bitter end.

Cementing our resistance to compromise is the apparent conclusion of activists on both sides (and probably correct), but especially on the side of pro-choice advocates, that an acquiescence on any one point would immediately be pounced upon by the other side to gain total victory. We are therefore locked in a deadly embrace, like two stags with their antlers irretractably intertwined, and there we stand, while time ticks on.

Yet, if we could put aside our volatile emotions for just a moment and consider the *consequences* of each proposed action, we might still be able to come to a compromise. But first, let's look at some facts, beginning with history.

History of Abortion in the United States

Abortion has been with us for as long as we have existed; we can trace it back at least some five thousand years. We know also that common-law societies have always considered it a private matter, better left up to the woman—that is, up until modern times. Things began to change in the U.S. around 1821, principally because of the medical profession's effort to control irregular medical practitioners, who at the time included pharmacists, homeopaths, surgeons, and midwives. Midwives were known to be the chief suppliers of chemicals used to induce abortion, and the laws passed seemed more directed towards them, as well as pharmacists, than towards abortion. Nevertheless, in spite of these laws, and a slew of others passed between 1840 and 1860, abortion continued at roughly the same rate as before.

Over the next hundred years or so abortion was carried out either illegally or by sympathetic physicians, usually under a broad interpretation of the legal exception for "therapeutic" abortions.[1] After 1945, however, hospitals became part of the decision process. Then in 1962, the thalidomide-deformed births, and later the rubella epidemic of 1966 in San Francisco, threw the issue to the forefront, bringing public attention to the need to re-address the laws concerning abortion.

Around this time many women began to unite and call for repeal of abortion laws, asserting they were an infringement on the inherent and fundamental right of a woman to decide on matters concerning her own body. De facto unfairness was also cited. It was pointed out that abortion laws drove many women of lessor socioeconomic standing to illegal and dangerous abortion practitioners, while their more affluent peers were always able to find a doctor or a hospital for a safe abortion.

Another group arose, adamantly opposed to abortion at any time for any reason. This was their theoretically ideal position, although most were willing to compromise when the life of the pregnant woman was in danger. They considered abortion to be homicide and called for laws to prohibit it as well as provide punishment for anyone involved (except for the pregnant woman).

This is basically how the two extremes squared off against each other. Many non-extremists felt the need to take one of these positions merely to prevent the other from prevailing.

Roe v. Wade

In 1973, the Supreme Court took on the controversy, issuing its landmark decision in Roe v. Wade. In effect, abortion was removed from the arena of illegality and a woman's right to privacy was upheld, grounded in the Ninth and Fourteenth Amendments, and defined to also encompass her decision on whether or not to terminate a pregnancy. The Court held also that "the pregnant woman can not be isolated in her privacy."[2] It conceded our inability to define precisely when human life begins and outlined when the state could step in to protect potential human life. The logical division of trimesters in human embryo/fetus development was used to delineate: (1) when the state could in no way interfere (first trimester), (2) when it could interfere only to protect the woman's health (second trimester), and (3) when it could intervene to protect potential and viable life (last trimester).

Never Say Die

In spite of the Supreme Court's decision, strife continues. Federal and state legislatures fight tooth and nail over every public expenditure connected in any way with abortion. In the courts antiabortionists wage continuous battle to reverse Roe v. Wade. In the streets they demonstrate, and in front of abortion clinics they lurk militantly, attempting to intimidate away pregnant women and clinic employees.

Convinced theirs is a fight for the highest ideals possible, and that God is on their side, they are determined to have their way, without regard for or recognition of the consequences. Pro-choice organizations, in turn, respond with both counter-demonstrations and counter propaganda, so as not to lose ground already gained. Consequently, the issue remains in a continual loop—reform, repeal of reform, reform, repeal of reform, ad infinitum. We stand powerless to advance to the next level and direct our energies towards *reducing* the call for abortion, achieving better birth control and pre-natal care, and reducing the circumstances that cause women to resort to abortion. Instead, we delay improving the human condition, and stifle genuine debate, by resurrecting the old battles, not on the grounds that more has been learned since Roe v. Wade, but simply because antiabortionists continue to fume and rage.

The Moral High Ground

We've now looked at some history and we've stated the problem. How can we solve it? A simple and solid first step would be to agree that this subject is far too intricate to approach without our emotions under control. For every horrible image of an aborted fetus, there exists an equally disturbing one of a woman suffering torturous death from a botched self-attempt at abortion, or at the hands of an injurious and incompetent black-market practitioner. For every happy family lovingly devoted to their deformed child, there is another family perplexed beyond their ability to cope. For every line of prose bathing us in God's cozy love, there is the reality of a family living in squalor—reduced to an animal-like existence until the day they die.

Let's examine for a moment the strongest influence on prevailing emotions—religious conviction. History, we must agree, shows us that religious zeal has been far from synonymous with humane treatment here on earth. One need only look at the masses sacrificed to holy wars, at the immense suffering caused by the inquisition, at the burning and breaking of heretics, and at the offerings of human sacrifice, to see what occurs when life's purpose is construed merely for the praise or pleasing of God. More than a little pain, suffering, and death has occurred in praise of deities.

But even putting aside historical cruelties and injustices, there is no justification for insisting that one's own religious or moral views be imposed on all. This is an audacity, not a solution. Of course, we all have the right to our own convictions but not the right to inflict those convictions on others. Isn't that the *meaning* of religious freedom. Can we honestly expect anyone to permit personal moral matters to be decided for him or her by others, especially by those not destined to live with the consequences? And, obviously, it's a lot easier to feel emotionally good about a position when conveniently ignoring the consequences of that position.

So where does all this leave us? One conclusion is that we cannot devise reasonable laws for *all* to live under based on the religious views of some; religion cannot be the basis for legislating social behavior. On the other hand, nascent life *is* involved, life which also has a right to protection. This is the dilemma we face. It is more a moral perplexity than a legal one, but that is not to say there is nothing we can do to protect this life by law.

Abortion may be the most difficult moral dilemma mankind has ever faced and will continue to require a lot of effort, study, and soul-searching, yielding only to small increments of improvement, connected directly to human intellectual and moral advancement. That having been said, it's time to discuss the *consequences* of each course thus far proposed.

Absolutely No Abortion

What would result if laws were passed prohibiting abortion entirely? What has always been the outcome of laws not agreed upon by a substantial number of the population? Abortions would not stop; that is certain. We have proof of that. Those with means and sophistication would, as always, find their way to medically safe abortions. The rest would be consigned to the hands of underground practitioners, who would proliferate, together with the cases of horror and death that always accompany them. Anyone still not convinced need only look back in U.S. history at the futile attempt to prohibit the sale and manufacture of alcohol —an illuminating example of what happens when ideology is used to legislate. Of course it failed miserably. Until it was finally repealed it was both an affront to those who could decide for themselves whether to drink, or how much to drink, and the direct cause of an immense black market, with rampant associated crime. What better example could we have? Obviously, it is total folly to pass laws without a moral consensus to support them.

The consequences of laws forbidding abortion are therefore clear. Before leaving the matter, however, there is another point at issue—the implication such laws would have for our concept of human liberty. Interference by the state in *forbidding* abortion is every bit as oppressive as the state *enforcing* abortion, such as has occurred under oppressive Chinese regimes. Both prohibiting and mandating abortion have in common the devaluing of individual autonomy. Democracies have always become more democratic by valuing individual autonomy, only legislating against it when necessary. Totalitarian governments, on the other hand, have always devalued individual autonomy. Which do we want?

Absolutely No Abortion Laws

What about frivolous abortion, abortion because of the sex of the child, or abortion simply on demand, with complete disregard of the fetus? These are, of course, clear circumstances where the state *must* step in to protect nascent life from unreasonable action of others. And obviously, the more developed embryonic life is, or the more frivolous the reason, the greater must be our concern and our vigilance.

The Absolute Solution

Having faced and discussed the consequences, we could then direct our efforts towards solution. There actually is one within grasp. The solution is to *accept* the prevailing consensus-driven compromise, while continuing to debate and work for improvement, but with persuasive argument, not brainless demonstrations.

The present consensus, whether antiabortionists like it or not, is that in early pregnancy the choice, the moral decision, cannot be taken from the woman. In the late stages of pregnancy, or when there are frivolous reasons, there is equal consensus that the state has the obligation to intervene on the part of the fetus. Isn't it wiser to build on these than to ignore them? Doing so will not move us closer to abortion as a means of birth control, nor will it induce unwarranted encroachment by the state into the woman's right of control over her own body. It will, however, give us a reasonable, rational way to live together while we continue to explore and refine our own values and persuade others to adopt them.

There is an immense middle, gray area upon which we can and should logically focus. We need to continue the debate on when the fetus is a human being and therefore under the laws protecting human life. With equal consideration for both the fetus and the woman, we need to weigh the rights that belong to each. But we cannot allow extremists to throw us back into the dark ages of rampant illegal and dangerous abortions. Neither can we move toward treatment of fetuses as mere excretions of the body.

Most of us understand abortion is not a pleasant or desirable thing—not something to be taken lightly as, for example, another form of birth control. When done, it is best done as soon as possible. It is time for us to also understand that abortion is first and foremost a moral problem, a very *personal* moral problem, and no one suffers emotionally more than the woman deciding for it. It is not murder for her to have an abortion, but in her swirl of emotions, this may be something with which she charges herself. Assuming our goal is to actually resolve this issue, not forever war over it, each side must begin to give the other some credit for also being reflective and humane. Maybe then we could progress towards the best solution currently possible, given the state of our knowledge, by intelligently discussing and debating potential laws that would provide the most protection of a woman's right to control over her own body, and at the same time protect nascent life from irresponsible termination. Diametrically opposed "rights to life" are involved. To pass a law that secures *only* the rights of one would naturally infringe on the rights of the other. The solution is therefore to apply restraint, instituting laws that infringe as little as possible on either, while leaving it, as much as possible, a personal moral decision.

In the meantime, as well as in the aftermath, it would be a far better use of our energies to work at discouraging abortion: by offering pre- and postnatal health care, by better providing for adoption, and, in short, by doing everything we can to make birth something to be looked forward to. And we should start soon, for even more difficult decisions face us in the future, as the onslaught of biological and technological advances begin to blur the lines of morality. And it is here that we can benefit the most from the continued—but constructive—vigilance of the right-to-lifers, in protecting the fetus and guarding against any creeping excesses.

A clear foundation for compromise lies before us in the Supreme Court's decision, but we will need something more. Ultimate solution—as with all of our societal problems—lies in the rapid development of a more literate and reasoning public. Such a population would, in fact, need few laws on abortion; it would be a serious enough matter for them, as individuals, to decide and face for themselves. Without, however, a radical turnabout in the manner in which we view education, there can be no hope of reaching such a state and therefore little hope of dealing successfully with this and other issues, as we are about to discover.

*These things shall be! A loftier race
Than e're the world hath known shall rise,
With flame of freedom in their souls,
And light of knowledge in their eyes.*
—John Addington Symonds

Chapter 3

Race Relations

Can We Talk? (as Joan Rivers was fond of asking)

The answer is no, we can't talk. It's not politically correct. Even if it were, it's doubtful we could have useful discussion, judging from the current discourse, off on a track by itself, heading nowhere and accomplishing nothing. Why? Because it studiously avoids any criticism of black actions or black attitudes.

Before attempting honest discussion on race relations, however, let's pause again to briefly review history. Everyone knows by now that blacks were originally brought to this country against their will, enslaved for two and a half centuries, and even after emancipation, not given full rights and protection under the law. Unfair, cruel, brutal, and murderous treatment lasted well into the 1960s. Blacks were discriminated against in jobs, housing, public facilities, and school opportunities, and as a consequence occupied a much lower socioeconomic position than whites.

What everyone does not seem to recognize is that our indulgence in a 28-year national guilt trip, trying to right the big wrong, is not rectifying the situation. In fact, given our limited ability to debate, we have managed to befoul racial relations all over again. This time we've swung too far to the pro-black side, creating an atmosphere where "prejudice" is assumed to lay behind every black shortcoming, and allowing every black caught red-handed, to play the "race card" with impunity, and often success, but never with rebuke.

As the white majority wallows in past guilt, blacks have settled into a continuous celebration of "blackhood", ignoring the need for self-improvement and giving little attention to the struggle for our common future. Almost every world event (Gulf War), national event (election, presidential appointment), and national issue (education) becomes an opportunity for black spokesmen to champion black causes or charge discrimination, with Jesse Jackson as self-appointed "free safety".

In addition, we continue to acerbate the total situation and hinder development of correct racial relations, with the misguided and antiproductive government policy of Affirmative Action. What exactly is this policy and where did it come from? Again, some history.

Affirmative Action

In 1964 the Civil Rights Act was passed, putting an end to long-standing practices of racial segregation and discrimination, practiced against blacks in public services and employment. Executive Order 10925 of 24 September 1965, signed by Lyndon Johnson, put into effect *Affirmative Action*, requiring all federal agencies and anyone wishing to do business with the federal government to prove compliance with the Civil Rights Act and show that: "... applicants are employed, and that employees are treated during employment, without regard to their race, creed, color, or national origin. Such action shall include, but not be limited to the following: employment, upgrading, demotion, or transfer; recruitment or recruitment advertising; layoff or termination; rates of pay or other forms of compensation; and selection for training, including apprenticeship." Public notification of employer compliance was also required. The term *Affirmative Action* was used within this Executive Order to describe the requirement of federal agencies and would-be government contractors, and their subcontractors, to *affirm* their compliance.

For many, the way to gain de facto proof of compliance, thereby "affirming" their compliance, was to immediately employ a representative amount of blacks. Thus came into being the establishment of special treatment in hiring blacks for the civil service and elsewhere. This action, of course, directly contradicted the Civil Rights Act, since it was definitely *making use of race* in hiring practices. All of this, nonetheless, was carried out in the spirit of bootstrapping blacks and other minorities up to a higher socioeconomic status, thereby speedily rectifying past injustices.

Since then, with the help of Supreme Court decisions, Affirmative Action has settled into the more or less accepted practice of granting special treatment to minorities, especially blacks. That special treatment constitutes granting government contracts, work positions, and school and university places, to minorities of lower qualifications than their competitors.

This brings us not only up-to-date on Affirmative Action but straight to some important questions. What has been the effect of this policy to date? Should we keep it? Is it serving to eliminate racial conflict or is it causing more polarization? What *does* work in eradicating racial discrimination and in improving relations, and what does not? Where do we go from here?

The Effects of Affirmative Action

To evaluate its total impact we must examine the effects of Affirmative Action on both blacks and the nation.

Affirmative Action and the Black Community

There is no doubt Affirmative Action has been a boon to many individuals; it cannot be argued, however, that it has improved the situation of the *majority* of blacks in America. Black illiteracy still rampages ahead of the rest of the country and a disproportionate number of blacks occupy the lowest rungs of our society.

The supposition supporting Affirmative Action was that, as soon as blacks were given jobs, everything else would follow and fall into place. More and better education would ensue and greater understanding between the races would develop, by virtue of working and living side by side.

Some of the latter has occurred, with Affirmative Action undoubtedly playing a role in wearing down long-standing pillars of prejudice. Still, Affirmative Action cannot be judged a success. Its chief goal and benefit—education—has failed to emerge. If it had, we would have long ago reversed a policy of granting special privileges to one segment of the population. There would be no need to.

Furthermore, this policy of granting special privileges has had a corrosive effect on the nation as a whole, while continual preoccupation with black pride has hindered, not aided, the progress of black education.

Black Education

No one can dispute that increased ability to use language correlates to increased mental ability. To put it another way, the greater the vocabulary, the greater the ability to conceptualize, to form and express ideas, to think. The more correctly and precisely vocabulary is used, and the more accurate the thinking process, the better the chances of being understood and influencing others. There simply can be no doubt of the importance of language. Neither does anyone dispute that the working language in the United States is English.

In spite of both these verities, there is noticeably little attention given by black families or the black community towards improving black use of the language. To the contrary, an inferior version of English (with slave-time remnants such as: "I be, dey, dat, wif", and so on) if not encouraged, is accepted, as a matter of black identity. Even worse, a lazy drawl running words together into one long moan is commonly accepted speech. (A similar criticism can be leveled at the population as a whole. The point is that it must never be encouraged or supported. Clearness of speech demands distinction between words and syllables.)

The tacit justification for this attitude is that this manner of speaking embodies black identity and culture. This, of course, is a grievous mistake. The only identity preserved is that of a former slave. Nevertheless, if blacks still wish to preserve this manner of speaking, it can and should be retained as a second language.

Do members of other ethnic groups—Indians, Italians, Japanese, for example—wishing to be assimilated into U.S. society, fail to adopt English? They obviously strive with the first generation and succeed with the second to speak the same language as everyone else. For them it is an important and obvious step towards having an equal chance at everything. Many retain their former languages and ties to their former culture, but that doesn't prevent them from learning English. Blacks could do the same and many do. But a significant number ridicule dual language blacks as hypocrites and opportunistic imitators of whitey. Again, they adopt the argument that such action undermines black culture and black identity.

This unfortunate attitude is a gross error, which virtually no one speaks out against. Progress, whether for a nation, a race of people, or an individual, comes only with learning, and language is clearly as important for learning as anything can be. Yet it appears for the majority of blacks, proficiency in language has either been neglected or discouraged. And when an entire group of people follow a path counter to national purpose, the nation has a duty to criticize and attempt correction.

In addition, an inordinate amount of black education is directed towards bolstering pride in black achievements, to the neglect of other information. Again, this has not been a preoccupation of other ethnic groups landing in the U.S. They have focused education on the future not the past. Granted, they arrived under much different circumstances, but regardless of past events, the current *trip* of euphoria over everything black is a self-indulgence that is helping no one. It does little, if anything, for black children. Real pride and self-esteem comes through learning more of everything, and real learning requires the ability to be self-critical. Imagine how little a speaker, as often featured on black radio, can contribute to racial pride or advance understanding on any issue, when he is only able to communicate with "uhs" and "ahs" and the frequent "You understand what I'm sayin?"

History is an important part of education, but it consists of much more than the story of any one nationality or race. There may indeed be need to rectify the withholding of deserved credit from minorities in white-written history, but this is less important to everyone, including blacks, than moving forward and solving today's problems.

Black Attitudes

Unearned rewards produce predictable results. Simply being handed something, automatically depreciates its value in the eyes of the attainer. This is especially true for a job granted on any basis other than qualification; both effort level and job performance suffer. Incentive is destroyed and replaced by an attitude which not only seeks to justify existing privileges but demands more and more. An example can be seen within the many federal agencies in Washington, D.C., where the dominant employee is black and female. Some are apparently unaware of or uninterested in following basic telephone answering conventions. Nor do they extend any effort to improve their diction and speak so they can be understood. The obvious impression one gets is that there is no concern at all in correcting this or, if there is, no one dares or cares to make the effort.

This was not difficult to predict. Anyone would react the same. If a job is handed to you and nothing more than minimal effort is required, minimal effort is all you will give. Your ambition, if any, will merely be to obtain more privileges.

Anyone ever attending a minority-business convention has witnessed this attitude first hand. There is less discussion on how to improve business techniques or personnel training, more discussion on how to keep privileges and fight off opponents to continuing non-competitive contract awards. Most disturbing of all, star speakers such as Gus Savage (former congressman from Chicago) brazenly orchestrate black racism, blasting everyone non-black, all the while supported by a chorus of "amens" from the audience.

This brings us to possible repercussions inherent in the present situation. There is growing danger that the *reverse discrimination* of Affirmative Action will eventually evoke reaction. The frustration is there, but there is no one to articulate it and no forum to discuss it. Nonetheless, tolerance of one-sided racism must eventually wear thin. Today, blacks engage almost daily in public racist talk on black radio and, whenever a black candidate is offered, most often their vote is strictly racial, regardless of the candidate's qualifications vis-à-vis the others. As jurors, they have been known to unabashedly set free criminals out of racial sympathy.[1] Such actions by whites are rightly condemned as racist but, in our present climate, are accepted from blacks.

The prevailing attitude of the majority in the country can be likened to that of a man who has mistreated his weaker spouse and now, out of feelings of regret, is allowing her to vent her anger by slapping him continuously. Such a situation cannot continue indefinitely. Either the slapping stops and communication begins or the slapping is forcefully halted and the danger of renewed violence arises.

* * *

Already from what has been said thus far, it is clear that Affirmative Action has done little for blacks as a people, not having helped to achieve real education, while at the same time negatively influencing black attitudes. Rather than entering the mainstream, striving for total improvement, blacks have more often opted to promote only black causes, to the point of losing credibility, a credibility which suffers most from the almost total absence of self-criticism. Although a disproportionate number of blacks are illiterate, account for crime, and are recipients of social programs, the blame is *always* placed totally elsewhere. There is little or no acknowledgment of the need for black improvement.

In contrast, individual blacks competing equally *without* Affirmative Action, as in business and athletics, have done the most to counter prejudice and prove their ability to compete on a level playing field. Their success demonstrates that people can easily disregard race, and like and respect each other, when they are dependent on each other's skills and knowledge for their mutual benefit.

Affirmative Action and the Country

To complete our evaluation of Affirmative Action we must also address its effect on the rest of the nation, which has been more negative than positive. In addition to increasing racial polarization it has accelerated our decline. Rather than upraising one segment of the population to a higher level of competence and attainment, as was intended, the net result has been to lower overall standards, competence levels, and accomplishments. Contrary to encouraging initiative, education, and sweat as values that bring success, it has done the opposite, helping accelerate our economic plunge. Only recently have we finally begun to realize the extent of decline in our competence, competitiveness, and education, as we stand watching Japan and Germany surge ahead of us.

This is *not* to say that blacks, or any single group, is at fault for our rapid deterioration. The fault lies in our failure at education. It is clear, however, that the method we have chosen to rectify past racial injustices is not working. Contrary to leveling the playing field for everyone, regardless of race, we have leveled it, regardless of competence.

The Verdict on Affirmative Action

We see now, if we look honestly, Affirmative Action is not serving the majority of blacks and it is not operating for the betterment of the country; therefore, it is not working. Quick fixes seldom endure. What *will* work is to ensure everyone the same opportunity at education and insist on performance as the basis of reward. And how do we do this?

Before answering, let's be certain of one thing: it's either adjust society to be completely equal-handed, or see it torn apart. Clearly, there's little future for any of us in a world of racial warring. And only by truly applying the constitution to all will we reach stability and racial equilibrium in the U.S. Affirmative Action is currently an obstacle to this progress, but we seem incapable of even discussing it, or too cowardly. It is even doubtful, given our ineptness at discussion and debate, that, until education finally arrives, such a volatile and emotion-charged subject *can* be discussed without gross misunderstanding.

The real issue is not racial hatred. It's hatred for results the other race produces or encourages—oppression of minorities or perpetration of ignorance. We are past prejudgment based on skin color, hair texture, or facial features. The problem is behavior.

Someone such as David Duke would evoke reaction from only the lunatic fringe in a normalized atmosphere of open and honest exchange. But, today, he draws resonance simply by being the only one to speak into the current vacuum.

A good start towards bettering racial relations would be to insist on correct use of language by everyone. For example, it would be helpful to understand clearly and use correctly the terms "prejudice", "civil rights", "minority rights", "special rights", and "racial equality". There is no reason why "prejudice" should automatically be charged to someone criticizing attitudes, opinions, or practices of another race. And civil rights precludes the need for any other special rights, while racial equality demands that unjustified attacks on whites be equally condemned.

Progress towards racial harmony will also be greatly assisted by putting aside the past long enough to exchange honest criticisms, as well as discuss even-handedly proposals for eliminating racially-based problems. Present indulgence in timid and hollow discussions is getting us nowhere. On college campuses, for example, "political correctness" precludes any criticism of blacks and hence any open discussion. Throughout the country, fear of being labeled racist, forces everyone to bend over backward to devise and support ever new means of bolstering black self-awareness and self-respect. Consequently, we use our libraries, our schools, and, of course, our

Chapter 3 - Race Relations 53

TV shows to immerse ourselves in Black History, Black Perspective, and Black Identity. This is not only a posture too distorted to maintain, it is stunting our growth.

Here is an example of the harm and illogic of "political correctness":

A recent article in the Washington Post by John Rankine pointed out that the higher order skills or "the process of learning how to learn" were woefully lacking. True to form, from the sidelines objection was immediately raised in the form of the senseless argument that "the call for higher order thinking skills fails to address the problems of minority students in public schools... they [minorities and women] are severely under represented in mathematics and the sciences. Higher order thinking skills may represent one additional barrier for these students to hurdle."[2]

Such irrational and warped arguments make it clear why we are incapable of moving ahead towards education reform. Imagine, arguing against raising the level of education and performance for *all* of society on the grounds that "learning how to learn" would be "one additional barrier" for minority students to hurdle. Improving education is our most urgent task. We will be committing suicide for the entire nation, white and black, if we continue to foolishly fling about and accept the charge of racism as an obstacle to reforming education. Listen to the words of a representative teacher, as compiled by Paul Copperman in his book *The Literacy Hoax*:

C: How would you compare the level of skill of students today versus the early nineteen-sixties?
T: As I said, you can't compare. It's like comparing high-school students with junior-high students. The disparity is pretty enormous. I really think it has a lot to do with the level of teacher demands. Look at the racial thing. We've been bombarded for the last fifteen years with some kind of notion of what racism is. I know I've been very conscious of this. I've been bending over backward not to be identified as a racist who's going to come down hard on black kids. There's [sic] a lot of teachers who do the same thing. This translates into lower demands, if you teach in integrated classes, for everybody.[3]

And how do we react when confronted with these facts? Do we discuss them? No. Rather than meet the issue head on, public officials choose to talk in circles, concerned with how criticism of minorities will be perceived. Only criticism of whites is politically acceptable. Public discussion is therefore either totally one-sided, that is, black-sided, or so careful that actual progress is impossible. It is not surprising, therefore, that hateful shouts from society's fringe ring loudly in such a void.

Black public figures have also showed little desire to take the initiative. To be accurate there are a few, such as William Raspberry in his column for the Washington Post, who have pointed out the excesses of the black block in demanding forever special and non-competitive treatment, but so far no real discussion has ensued.

We can best summarize today's racial situation as a morass steadily becoming worse. Opportunities for improvement are lost every day, thanks again in large part to our miserable failure in education, but great success in anaesthetizing ourselves with entertainment. Surprisingly, even in our dazed condition, we still look to the future with hope, fantasizing that a great leader will arise and somehow guide us to reason. Where he will receive his education, though, is something few have considered.

Justly Into The Future

Notwithstanding all that has been said, good racial relations *are* attainable; required is simply honesty, forthrightness, and de-emphasis, rather than emphasis, of racial and ethnic differences.

We must, of course, continue to guarantee by law and practice, equal rights to everyone; however, this will require not only protection of rights, but also restraint from legislating or practicing preferential treatment, regardless of past injustices. In the future reward and success must go to those earning it by their abilities and efforts, not for any other reason.

It is therefore time to acknowledge that Affirmative Action, however well meant, is reverse discrimination and the wrong way to proceed. We must abandon it and in its place concentrate on additional training and educational help for those wanting and needing it, irrespective of race. *Education* must be our method for leveling the playing field; nothing else is equitable, long-lasting and effective.

It is also entirely rational for the nation to concentrate on quality of performance rather than "correct" numerical proportions in the working force. Today's very competitive situation demands it. Employers need to hire the best, the most competent, no matter what the color. And businesses rejecting good people because of imbedded prejudice simply harm themselves. In fact, prejudice against skilled blacks or Asians, or Hispanics, or anyone, would be suicidal. The valuable "reject" would simply be hired by the competition. At the same time, however, successful businesses must sell both their products *and* the competence of their employees. Again, the importance of language: employees unable to use language effectively are obviously of little help, except in positions where language is minimally significant, such as manual labor.

We cannot get away from the truth that command of the language is fundamental to everyone's progress, an indispensable tool for every occupation or profession. But even aside from its economic importance, our democracy itself depends on it. We think, therefore we are, to pluralize Descartes. Expressing it negatively, without language we cannot think and are therefore in danger of not existing. And interpolating to the present: with poor language, we think poorly, and therefore exist poorly.

There also can be no doubt that the first responsibility for language improvement lies within the family, regardless of family economics, and the slightest improvement guarantees to snowball in its effect. As parents we would not dream of sending our children out of the family and into the world without the ability to think; how can we casually release them into life's stream with *restricted* thinking capacity?

This may all be strikingly obvious, but where are our language proponents today? Where are the parents, neighbors, and teachers encouraging and emphasizing its importance? Many of us have perhaps abdicated this responsibility to the media, but the media simply adjust to the masses in order to reach the greatest audience. In the end, only the family, schools, and neighborhoods can place proper value on language.

Finally, we must look to the future and not the past. Certainly, we need to acknowledge past behavior, examine it, and understand it, but we will get nowhere by dwelling on the past. Anyone who reads world history knows of the enslavement and cruelties man has inflicted upon man, and there is virtually no race totally innocent of this behavior, nor any that has escaped its victimization. It's simply not a private trait of any one nation or race. The past is full of atrocities. Convoluting life today, however, in an effort to make up for them, is simply foolish. We cannot correct the past; we can only proceed justly into the future.

We must therefore cease circling around critical issues affecting racial relations and meet them head-on like intelligent human beings. By continuing to suppress good-faith, intelligent discussion, we simply allow hatemongers on both sides to speak for us. We could, for example, begin by *defining* and *articulating* what we do want in the way of race relations in a just society, and what we do not want. Once this is discussed publicly and truthfully, the way would be prepared to move ahead towards achieving what we all agree to achieve.

It is clear as a nation, all of us, regardless of our race, are falling behind economically and socially. If we are to recover and regroup for the future, we need both the energy to apply strenuous and honest thinking and the courage to stand up for reason. If we continue as we are, there can be no doubt about our fate; history will record that the New World eventually ran its course, fading into the shadows after only a few centuries, unable to deal with the cultural diversity it had both created and attracted.

Chapter 4

Crime and Violence

It's difficult to apply a ranking to our national problems, but crime and violence, taken together, must be near the top. No one can escape its reach. From the richest to the poorest, the youngest to the oldest, the highest office of the land to the lowest, we all live in the permanent shadow of its threat.

It is also the most widely publicized of our activities. News coverage is filled daily with its tragedies, played out in our cities, our suburbs, and even our rural areas. Violent crime has become a permanent part of our culture and, in fact, could be labeled our national pastime. It certainly is the major ingredient of our entertainment. Nowhere else in the world is gruesome, bloody mayhem and mutilation enjoyed more as entertainment than in the U.S. We thrive on it. We even honor Hollywood for its expertise in presenting it—for simulating severed heads, squirting blood, and exploding guts—and speak of the construction of horror characters as if their creation were a work of art and a worthwhile accomplishment. No doubt there will someday be an academy award for the most gross, gore-filled and horrifying "special effects of the year".

Unbelievable as it may sound, though, we excel in actual crime even more than the Hollywood version. Everyone is aware of our accomplishments in fire-arm violence. In fact, we are rapidly leaving the civilized world behind and returning to our glorious days of the wild west. Washington D.C. resembles more a lawless frontier territory, trying to clean itself up enough to obtain statehood, than it does a modern capital city. Even congressmen and congresswomen, with their secured underground passageways, cannot totally escape the violence, although they are, of course, more afraid of the NRA.

Crime and violence are slowly but steadily overwhelming—while simultaneously and pathetically entertaining—us and this has been going on for decades. Already in 1970 it was four times as dangerous (considering only homicides) to live in Detroit than it was to live in strife-torn Belfast, Northern Ireland.[1] Since then, the figures have gotten steadily worse.

Gun Control and the NRA

The role of the handgun in U.S. crime could not be more obvious, as is that of its equally dangerous partner, the assault weapon—as clear to see today as the correlation of cigarette smoking with cancer. Nevertheless, special-interest groups, especially the NRA, have successfully blocked every attempt to introduce national controls and halt their proliferation. And never have more illogical arguments been put forth in public than those used against proposed gun registration laws. Starting with the remonstrance that "guns don't kill people, people do", the NRA and their proponents go on to argue against restrictions on assault weapons because

    a) they are legitimate sporting weapons
    b) collectors should be free to collect them

If left to the NRA every man, woman, and child would be armed to the teeth as protection against potential invading hoards of Communists, Martians, Huns, or whatever else is out there to shoot. But, contrary to the NRA and its adherents, Americans are not overwhelmingly interested in freely buying and using guns. Those desiring and needing unrestricted access to guns are the criminals. It would not be surprising to find every criminal in the land enrolled in, and fully supporting, the NRA; it would help account for their enormous membership.

Although it's true, registration laws will never totally prevent hardened criminals from obtaining guns, it is equally true that the ready access, practiced in our society, makes it a lot easier for drug rings and street gangs to operate, and for the mentally disturbed to act out their delusions. A few statistics should help us focus on the extreme menace of handguns. In 1990, out of 20,045 murders 12,847 were accomplished with guns.[2] That's over 64 percent. More recent data show 24,703 murdered in 1991—the worst yet— and the number one reason cited is the steadily increasing availability of handguns.[3]

There simply can no longer be any reasonable doubt about the close association of homicide with readily available handguns. As proof, let's go back some eleven years to 1981, when murder had already claimed twice as many U.S. citizens as those killed in all U.S. wars combined.[4] Already then, we were killing each other at a rate ten times that of any other advanced western civilization, with 50 percent of the homicides involving blacks killing blacks. Handguns were used in 70 percent of crimes, and 98 percent of policeman slain were killed by guns.

In spite of those statistics, a spokesman (Research Coordinator) for the NRA stated that there was "no relationship between the availability of guns and murder."[5] He also countered with his own loose statistics, declaring there were four to eight million cases (what a range!) where guns were used successfully in defense. Was he talking about wars, movies, novels or what?

One could double over with laughter at the absurdity of the NRA's position were it not successful. Of course, their efforts have enjoyed the benefit of dealing with minds that prefer simplistic answers and "toys for big boys" to anything as uncomfortable as reasoning. But the secret of their power lies elsewhere. It emanates from control of an enormous campaign contribution chest and the ability to launch unequaled letter-writing campaigns that leave congressmen trembling in fear of the silver bullet. It's that simple. Even after public polls showed 85 percent of gun owners (not to mention the National Fraternal Order of Police) were in favor of restrictions on the sale of handguns and assault weapons, congress still obtrusively refused to pass any such legislation. (As mentioned, congress cares little about what John Q. Public thinks, knowing they can purchase his vote with money received from the NRA.)

Let's take a moment to examine the latest national attempts to apply some brakes to the slaughter. In May, 1991 the Brady bill began life with a 239-186 passage in the House but later died the usual death of legislation designed to help the majority, but in opposition to monied interest. (Full account of the life and death of the Brady and anti-crime bills is contained in the Chapter Notes.)[6] Here is a post-mortem look at two of the simple measures that were being proposed:

1) To require a seven-day waiting period, in order for a police check to be made, before the purchase of a handgun.
2) To prohibit the sale and manufacture of specific assault weapons.

The opposition to this bill relied on the NRA's same tiresome arguments:

a) Making people wait seven days is in violation of their constitutional "right to bear arms".
b) Guns don't kill people, people do.
c) Gun control is not crime control.
d) If you start with *controlling* one type of gun, soon all guns will be *taken away*.
e) Gun control just takes weapons from law-abiding citizens; criminals can always get guns.

Chapter 4 - Crime and Violence 61

    f) Assault weapons are legitimate hunting guns [police hunting?].
    g) Gun collectors need access to assault weapons, therefore their manufacture and sale cannot be prohibited.

(Tell me Sir, you've led a life of violent crime—murder, armed robbery, assault with a deadly weapon—what would you call yourself, I mean in what profession are you? Whata ya think, Ima gun collector!)

As we all know, the opposition won.

This scene has been repeatedly played out before us for years. In fact, this single issue, better than any other, best exposes the cynicism and hypocrisy infesting our congress. There is absolutely no basis for opposing this legislation other than selfish concern for NRA money. None. (The fact that the crime bill was eventually packed with other controversial measures was also within Congress's power to prevent.) Congressman Les AuCoin finally acknowledged this ignominy, saying: "... I discovered what an ideological straightjacket that NRA seal of approval can be... — the leadership of the NRA has made its congressional supporters patsies in a game of lethal consequences."[7] And even Ronald Reagan, who lacked the wisdom and the courage to do so as president, finally came out in support of national gun control measures. No matter, the NRA has continued to prevail.

(The NRA's own proposal for handgun registration must, of course, be mentioned. They proposed the implementation of a huge and *expensive* (future) computer system, which would make background checks and grant approval within minutes, instead of forcing anyone to wait *seven whole days* to get a handgun. It was an obvious attempt to diffuse and confuse some of the strong arguments beginning to get through.)

But let's finish our examination of the issue. Beyond the obvious lack of merit in the NRA's arguments there were, and still are, these facts to consider:

a) Gun runners make a living by traveling down to Virginia, where they can readily obtain handguns, transporting them back to New York City, and selling them to criminals at a profit.
b) New Jersey's mandatory background check, required before a handgun can be purchased, has caught over 10,000 convicted felons trying to purchase handguns.
c) A seven-day wait for a handgun, although terribly inconvenient, doesn't keep guns out the hands of law-abiding citizens. It does, however, keep them out of the hands of felons, junkies, and the mentally disturbed.
d) Sixty Americans die from handgun violence each day.
e) More teenage boys now die from gunshot wounds than from all natural causes put together.
f) Adolescent suicide attempts in the U.S. are 75 percent successful if there is a gun in the house, whether it's locked up or not. Adolescent suicide attempts are only 25 percent successful when any other means is used.

These facts, however, do not daunt the opposition. As counter attack they argue that gun registration infringes on the citizen's constitutional right to bear arms. And here we are presented with a clear insight into our lack of sophistication in debating. Putting aside for a moment the fact that *registering* handguns is not the same as *taking away* handguns, let's look at what Amendment 2 of the constitution says: "A well regulated militia, being necessary to the security of a free State, the right of the people to keep and bear arms, shall not be infringed."

Obviously, the concern of the founding fathers was that the country would have the capability to supplement its military in times of national emergency. Initially, the militia was drawn directly from the population and hence the need for an armed citizenry. National guard and reserve units now constitute our present-day militia, and they are both armed and trained. The founding father's intent is still in place. In spite of the great disappointment it may cause some gun-toting Americans, they are no longer considered our militia unless, of course, they join the National Guard or reserves. Even in the Guard or reserves, however, *personal* weapons have no place. Obviously, the fear of many gun lovers is that they will somehow lose their right to own them. Their reaction to this fear, however, is reminiscent of a pouting child sticking its fingers in its ears, refusing to listen to anything. No one advocates totaling denying gun ownership. At issue is the attempt to deny ownership to criminals and the mentally disturbed, as well as elimination at the source of those weapons that allow criminals and the mentally deranged to multiply the number of their victims ten- and twenty-fold.

To conclude: there is no credible reason for Congress not to unanimously pass handgun control legislation, as one small step towards stemming the tide of crime. They do not. They will not. As long as their reelection hinges, not on responsible actions, but on money available for TV commercials, why should they?

Gun control, however, is not our only issue under the category of crime and violence in America. Let's move on to more.

Our Judicial System

Next to proliferation of handguns, which we have proved powerless to stop, we suffer from a defect-laden judicial system. First, it is extremely haphazard in its administration, and second, like politics, it is enormously influenced by money, or lack of it.

There is nothing consistent about our laws and sentencing and, with fifty states each having their own judicial and penal systems, that's to be expected. But the variables influencing convictions and sentencing go well beyond differences in state laws, and include such things as availability of prison space, prejudiced and myopic juries, rampant sensational publicity, and, of course, the big one, money. We even allow our mania for entertainment to play a part. To get an idea of just how entertainment colors our judicial system examine this scenario which continually repeats itself.

1) A confessed serial killer murders a long list of victims in a particularly gruesome fashion, or alternately, a celebrity is caught red-handed in a criminal act.
2) The press proceeds to get maximum mileage out of the story, publishing daily the sensational details.
3) Major TV networks push the story to the front of the nightly news.
4) Publicity-hungry lawyers jostle to get the case, and then proceed to line up their defense of temporary insanity or, for the celebrated person, entrapment.
5) Negotiations begin immediately on book rights, TV mini-series rights, and film rights.
6) Defense lawyers use the predictable flood of publicity as an argument for the impossibility of finding impartial jurors.
7) Twelve unaware, uninformed, and without-opinion persons are found anyway.
8) Trial, media coverage, and news analysis focus on the game plan, play execution, and scoring ability of trial lawyers.
9) Everyone is entertained, many are enriched, and Lady Justice flees the scene in the midst of the commotion.

Meanwhile, crime continues unabated, thanks in no small part to the ubiquitous handgun. We can pick up the newspaper and in *one* day read:

"My Daddy Shot My Mommy"
"D.C. Man Fatally Shot in Car Near White House"
"Angry Japan Lays to Rest Student Shot Dead in U.S."[8]

(The latter was a sixteen-year-old exchange student who hadn't watched enough U.S. television to understand a gun-ready neighbor's shout to "freeze"). And for a summary of one week's local handgun news we can read:

"... gunman wearing a ski mask robbed a gas station ..."
"... argued with a man ... and shot him ..."
"... armed with a gun, robbed a news stand..."

"... unidentified man was found in a wooded area with a fatal gunshot wound to the head."
"... gunman robbed a laundry business..."
"... armed with a gun stole a blue 1987 Subaru..."
"... gunmen robbed a tire business..."
"... gunman ... robbed a convenience store ..."
"... gunman robbed a gas station..."
"... gunman robbed a convenience store..."
"... gunmen ... stole the 1992 Ford Explorer."
"... fatally shot while driving his car..."
"... sexually assaulted her at gunpoint."
"... shot a man walking toward an apartment building."
"... gunman robbed a fast-food restaurant..."
"... armed with a gun ... stole his electronic pager ..."
"... armed with a gun ... robbed a convenience store..."
"... armed with a gun ... robbed him of car keys and money."[9]

But we've already examined the handgun connection to our violent society; let's move on to examine the influence of money on our judicial system, especially in the tort arena.

First, one is intimidated off the scene if unable to match the legal budget of the opposing side. You may be in the right, but the opposing legal team, together with the system, can make it too expensive to pursue. Contingency fee to the rescue? Of course not. These arrangements are only employed when going after big bucks from insurance companies. In itself, the contingency fee is not a totally bad idea, but the manner in which it has been used in our system has been disastrous. Part of the problem lies in the enormous and unjustified court and jury awards, of which lawyers get an extremely high percent. And, of course, with over 45 percent of our Senate and House seats occupied by lawyers,[10] there has never been much interest in capping these excessive amounts.

Shall we look at libel suits? Here we find that *truth*, although the surest defense against a charge of libel, is often not used because the entire process can easily turn out to be both too expensive and time consuming. Not only is libel law slippery and complicated, it varies significantly from state to state. It's often less costly to simply settle; truth is too expensive.

Looking into probate law we see a beautiful example of a private money machine for lawyers. Observe how the ABA, other attorney associations, and federal judges, worked together to protect this gold mine when it was widely exposed by Norman F. Dacey in his book *How to Avoid Probate*. Even though, as Esperti and Peterson point out in their book *Loving Trust*, not all lawyers are scum and most in fact are not, the profession today, as it is currently practiced, presents one of the greatest threats to the future of the United States. It has already made us into a "cover your ass" society and skyrocketed the cost of everything connected with liability insurance. Its power and wealth derive not only from its disproportionate representation in our government, which allows it to block reform, but also from its unique positional advantage, from which it can create work and wealth for itself. For example, nearly fifty thousand government lawyers are engaged in the writing of laws, with as much legalese as possible, while many of the rest live off of contesting it. And money can buy a lot of assistance in discovering and exploiting the enormity of inconsistencies, holes, and technicalities, which can be used to, if not defeat justice, at least delay it forever.

Our legal system has developed into a deliberately complex and esoteric business, to the generous benefit of its ever-swelling number of practitioners (the U.S. supports *two-thirds* of all the lawyers in the world).[11]

Legal insurance itself works to encourage law suits; lawyers know insurance companies have money, but they aren't that certain of collecting from individuals. The end result of all this is that litigation today is extremely costly and "justice" excruciating slow. Everyone knows this but, as always, we are helpless to do anything about it.

Should the legal system serve as an arena for entrepreneurship and wealth building? Isn't its function more like that of a referee presiding over game participants? And isn't the sole *raison d'être* of its practitioners to understand the law and apply it with skill?

Assuming we all agree on the answers to these questions, it is incomprehensible that we continue to grant this profession a special license to *use* the law to build lavish personal wealth for its members, at the expense of everyone else. If immense wealth is what is sought, it's time for the members of the bar to change uniforms, step out onto the playing field, and compete for it fairly.

For some time now, we have permitted this profession to impose an enormous burden on the rest of the country, and our sole, feeble response has been to retaliate with anti-lawyer jokes. The jokes are funny, but obviously no match for the lure of money that perpetuates the problem. For a clear insight into the damage sowed we need only observe the actions of this profession that have helped to drive medical insurance costs through the roof. That, however, is a subject for Chapter 5, Health Care.

Obviously, we badly need reform of the legal profession, in general, and specific practices, in particular, and a suggested first step would be to put a strict curb on contingency fees. This, together with a cap on monetary damage awards (especially those with no relationship to actual damages), could be effective in reducing several drags on the economy, namely the cost burdens of unnecessary suits, and exorbitant insurance premiums. With no multimillion-dollar plums around to chase, the competition among legal firms could conceivably center on the most interesting and trial-worthy cases, the rest being left, as they should, to be pursued on a pay-as-you-go basis, if at all, and this particular rape of personal and national resources could finally come to an end.

Capital Punishment — Good or Bad?

As in abortion, the answer to this question continues to elude us, although we've had ample time and opportunity to gather information and study the matter. By now we ought to be able to evaluate the evidence, discuss it rationally and come to a conclusion. Instead, we find ourselves, similar to abortion, in a continuous-loop debate about capital punishment being moral or immoral, humane or inhumane, a deterrent or non-deterrent, with no notable progress.

Couldn't we simply break this issue down into segments and attempt to reach agreement in small, rational steps? ("Who should orchestrate these attempts to reach consensus?" you may ask.

Presumably, this is the chief reason we elect or appoint leadership.) A suggested first step could be to reach consensus on the ultimate goal of capital punishment. Presumably, it would be to accomplish

   a) a deterrent to murder
   b) the general protection of society

We could then proceed to the next step.

For example, the first question would obviously be: "is the death penalty a deterrent to murder?" The answer, equally obvious, is that deterrence is so deeply dependent on individuals, and their states of mind, that a general conclusion cannot be reached. In such an event, we would need to look at the individual circumstances of murder. In the case of murder for hire, it's easy to imagine the death penalty putting a damper on the supply of hired killers. In the case of murder from passion, however, we already know that probably nothing would serve as deterrent, since rational thought is not in command. The point is we could, by careful deliberation, come to conclusions on the effect of capital punishment on various types of murder.

Having looked at the issue of deterrence we could then look to the matter of protecting society. It seems likely the death penalty could be successfully argued for hideous and repeated crimes. The reasoning: persons perpetrating repeated murders, such as serial killers, show a basic enmity against society and are inclined to continue as a threat as long as they live. It also seems reasonable to select the death penalty for a remorseless and exceptionally cruel murder in which the perpetrator displays a detachment from normal feelings, feelings that prevent most of us from acting in such a way. Such a person, no doubt, continues to be a threat to others as long as he lives. On the other hand, someone who shoots a victim in the heat of a robbery is not necessarily a permanent threat to society and a candidate for execution.

At the same time, it would be equally wise to examine thoroughly the sentence to life imprisonment *without parole* as an effective method in accomplishing both goals.

Of course, none of this is new and such considerations as premeditation, mental capacity, and so on, are already part of the process. The point is that whatever general agreement we arrive at via national debate should be applied universally across the nation. Otherwise, we may never resolve this issue and others like it. Capital punishment cannot be construed as a matter for local jurisdiction. It is clearly a national issue, a constitutional "right-to-life" matter, or at least it should be.

Criminal Rehabilitation

It is assumed for this discussion that a criminal penal system exists for the purpose of deterring crime as well as initiating rehabilitation, to the extent reasonably possible, during incarceration. A successful penal system would therefore accomplish both purposes.

We know, in general, that our prisons have been overflowing their capacities for years, and that the present solution is often to simply release prisoners early, or place more on parole, in order to make room for the next. As a solution, one Attorney General has recommended increasing prison space nation wide. Asserting that the federal government successfully multiplied its prison space threefold in the eighties, he urges the states to do the same.[12] The recommendation is not of much use, however, since most states have no money at the moment to build new prisons.

Meanwhile, crime continues to rise, requiring ever more prison space. Even a rapid increase in prison space, however, would not solve our crime problems. For if we continually require more and more prison space we are obviously losing the battle anyway. Increased prison space alone cannot be a long-term solution.

Again, we could attack the problem by breaking down our approach into smaller steps. First, we might try to arrive at a consensus on what rehabilitation is. A suggested definition:

To rehabilitate is to

a) render a repeat of the criminal experience highly unattractive
b) release the person with an opportunity to be assimilated back into society

Incarceration for a sufficient time therefore makes sense and helps accomplish the first part of rehabilitation. It also makes sense to provide opportunity to learn or practice a trade during the time imprisoned. Otherwise, the time is wasted and step two of the rehabilitation process becomes more difficult, if not impossible.

But learning a new trade, applying an old one, or simply furthering one's education does not alone accomplish part two of the rehabilitation process. We must also make it universally possible for the ex-prisoner to re-enter society, and that means obtain employment.

Already there are volunteer organizations, acting as networks, to get such persons entry level jobs, based on the trust that's afforded the organization. Obviously, this is what a released prisoner needs. And unless there is someone or some organization willing to take the responsibility and stand up for him, as long as he deserves it, it is extremely difficult to imagine how anyone, no matter how well-intentioned, *could* make it back in. Hence our high rate of recidivism. After successful completion of a first job, however, the way would be clear for the ex-prisoner to reclaim his position in society. It occurs all the time, of course, with rock stars and sports figures. It seems, therefore, advisable to elevate this job placement activity out of the voluntary arena and make it a permanent part of the correctional system.

Police Brutality

To complete our sojourn into America's commonplace violence and rampant crime, let us attempt to examine, albeit briefly, this directly associated and very contemporaneous phenomenon. It is not surprising to find police brutality in a society that constantly entertains itself with violence, sees it as a thrill, and childhood curiosity about violence is understandable, being part of the curiosity about adulthood. But many of us apparently never outgrow this childlike fascination; it continues well into adult life, dominating our entertainment.

With daily sustenance throughout both childhood and adulthood, it is not surprising for violence to become deeply ingrained in the psyche of many. We can only guess that it affects some more strongly than others, and perhaps even more so those with little or no access to accepted emotional outlets, such as sports. These resultant *bad apples* enter all walks of life. Some join police forces where they continue to be bad apples, and if there are enough of them, or if the climate supports them, they soon make use of convenient opportunities to be cruel and violent and get away with it. Law enforcement often presents a perfect outlet for violent behavior and there is good argument that subconsciously violence-prone individuals are drawn to police work for just this reason.

In any case, at least part of the solution lies in ensuring that the climate is so charged against them that such individuals either discard their brutal inclinations or leave the police force. By climate, is meant of course the totality of both police leadership and individual attitudes.

There is, however, another contributor to the problem: police are the ones left to cope with the results of our judicial system failures and societal neglect. While we go merrily on with our individual lives, the burden of this particular negligence falls heavily on the police. They are the ones continually re-arresting dangerous offenders while the judiciary habitually releases them. They are the ones left dodging machine-gun bullets from every common criminal, while our campaign-fund hungry politicians kowtow to the NRA. Consequently, it is understandable for their frustration to also vent itself in the use of excessive force.

Regardless of how we look at it, the source of this problem can be traced eventually back to us, the majority, and our apathy. There is also absolutely no other solution but to correct our individual selves.

A Sobering Reflection

Many of us may feel we are still a lot better off living in the United States than other places in the world and therefore are not that concerned. Not so, however, for millions living in sections of our cities where they are in constant danger of losing their lives. The problem is very real and, as we have seen, some of its major contributing causes could not be more evident. Rampant crime and the inability to control handguns clearly go hand in hand, but even a more fundamental truth is before us: record-breaking violence must be expected in a society which values video entertainment far more than education.

Ramsey Clark's words on murder, in 1981, still ring true today.

> "... Murder is the ultimate human tragedy ... therefore it tells you quite a bit about the values, the interests, the concerns of a society when they're constantly intrigued by murder. It would be a happy place that was intrigued [instead] by the methodology of eliminating the possibility of murder." [13]

Chapter 5

Health Care

The Malady

The good news is that the quality of our health care is not all that bad. The bad news is we can't afford it. At least 37 million of us can't afford health insurance, and this number, up 42 percent in ten years, is swelling fast as medical costs soar out of control.

If any of the 37 million uninsured ever do need major medical care, the best they can hope for is the ordeal of being shuffled like a hot potato between public hospital emergency wards, each hospital attempting not to get caught with the whammy of a non-paying patient. In reality, a form of de facto national health care is already in place, albeit in a harsh and horrendously inefficient manner. Billions of dollars in hospital costs (an estimated eight billion in 1991) go unpaid each year. They are recovered by simply charging more from the insured patient, thereby driving up insurance premiums, and thereby forcing more into the pool of uninsured.

We're Number One

—in spending, that is. The U.S. spends more on medical care than any country in the world, $665 billion in a year (more than $2,500 for every man, woman, and child) and gets the least amount of health care for its money. For example, here's where we stand in infant care:

Country:	Rate*:	Year**:
The Netherlands	6	1991
Sweden	6	1989
Germany	6	1990
Taiwan	6.3	1989
Switzerland	6.9	1989
Canada	7.3	1989
Austria	8	1989
France	8.2	1989
Israel	9	1989
Belgium	9.4	1989
U.S.A.	9.6	1990

*comparative infant mortality rate figures per 1,000.
** taken from most recent sources available for the countries listed.

The infant mortality rate is commonly used to judge a nation's overall effectiveness in health care. These figures therefore succinctly sum up the *total* quality of our health care and cut through all of the hyperbole so often used to tell us how well off we are. We could also use another widely accepted gauge—the percentage of babies born with adequate weight. Here the U.S. trails twenty-three other nations.[1]

Of course, on the positive side, our laboratories, research facilities, and technology are the envy of the world and help us achieve better and better medical and surgical techniques. We are excellent in emergency and critical care, and sometimes miraculous in rescuing and artificially sustaining human life. This is glorious (and expensive) and simply great for a few. Meanwhile, the rest of us are gradually being totally shut out from health care. This exclusion is occurring in two ways. First, we are being priced out of health insurance. Many families and small businesses, already strapped by hard times, are totally unable to keep up with the huge premium increases, sometimes 50 percent, occurring year after year. The reasons for these tremendous increases we will look at in a moment. But there is yet another way we are being deprived of health care. With our strictly commercial approach to health insurance, those with a former or existing medical problem are finding themselves, more and more, unable to obtain insurance at all; they are fast becoming the lepers of our society. The few carriers still willing to insure these people are disappearing fast, and fallback emergency pools, created by state governments, are drying up rapidly. In addition to passive rejection many insurance companies are *actively* canceling policies, as a means of cutting costs and increasing profits, and few insurance carriers will guarantee the right of policy renewal.

And Sinking Fast

Economic Drag

Little has been said publicly of the effect of all this on our total economy, especially on the ability of U.S. firms to compete abroad, but it is significant. Small firms, which do us all the favor of employing one third of our total work force, suffer in their ability to attract talent, unable to match the health insurance offers of large firms. Only about one half can offer their employees any health insurance at all. Even persons on welfare refuse jobs which will not provide health insurance coverage, logically electing to stay on welfare in order to keep their Medicaid coverage.

Large firms are also buckling under the heavy burden they are expected to carry. The number paying full premiums for their employees steadily decreased in the 1980s, going from 37 percent in 1984 to 24 percent in 1988.[2]

Many of us are forced to forego career moves out of fear of losing our health insurance, or incurring a one to three year waiting period, or having to re-qualify. Add to this the effect on many occupations, such as bartender, beautician, hospital aide, musician, and so on, which are blackballed by many insurance companies as presenting *unwanted risks* or *instability*, and we can see what an inhumane and unfair system we have so tractably accepted, even to the point of handicapping our economic competitiveness.

Built-in Problem Accelerators

Intensifying our heath care quandary are factors built into the present system which guarantee to make it worse. We've already mentioned soaring costs, causing increased premiums, causing increased uninsured. This alone accounts for one third of the increase in premiums each year. Yet compounding this chaos, is the reality that there are *no checks and balances holding down medical charges*. Increases are simply declared by the medical care providers and passed on to the insurance companies, where they spiral upwards.

True, from time to time, insurance companies do put up resistance to the increased costs and attempt various means to check them, but in the end they simply raise their premiums, or put caps on what they will pay, or both. Even a limit on pay-outs constitutes no forceful brake on the medical profession or hospitals, since they simply hold the patient accountable for the rest, a practice referred to as "bill balancing". As the squabble over billing goes on between health care providers and insurance companies (not to mention the newly spawned profit center Health Care Cost Management Firms), each concerned with their own profits, we, the beleaguered public, simply pay more and more for less and less care.

Vulnerability

All non-millionaires are vulnerable. Our very existence is at the mercy of chance illness. Everything worked for, everything hoped for, can all be wiped out in one blow. Even if you are one of the fortunate ones insured through a large employer, there is no certainty that insurance will last. Putting aside lack of job assurance, there are the realities that: (1) many large firms are self-insured, (2) companies can and do go out of business, and (3) insurance companies can simply drop or cancel policies. We are all living on the shaky edge of disaster.

Deadlock and Despair

So here we are, a nation whose physical health is collapsing because we cannot afford our own care. How did we get to this stage? A good question and one worth taking time to think about. For over eighty years the majority of us have recognized the need for universal health care, but being easily manipulated by advertising, and appeals to emotion rather than reason, we have been easy to stave off. All it took was money and wise spending, and the AMA and insurance lobbies have the money. They've spent it on advertising, PR, and political campaign contributions—a combination that works unfailingly. The advertising and PR kept us emotionally afraid of change for fear of the bogey man "socialized medicine". The sizable political contributions ensured that, even if the propaganda was not totally effective, legislators would block any threats to the cause, regardless of how popular.

We have no right to be angry though. How else can we expect practical politicians to act? If, indeed, they should be so foolish as to vote what's good for the country, against the wishes of the money-offering special interests, they risk almost certain termination of their political careers.

They need not fear criticisms of their lack of ethics either, since they can easily throw out any number of nonsensical arguments as immediate damage control. These are hardly ever challenged, at least not by enough to make any difference. Even the press is of little help, as journalist and their editors prefer to uncover new problems rather than hammer away at long-existing ones.

For over fifty years we have acquiesced to the AMA, the insurance companies, and their paid-for congressman, allowing them to maintain a system which primarily serves them, not us. As a consequence, our commercial approach to health care now inherently excludes those unable to pay the ever rising premiums or who make the mistake of once getting a blemish on their health record. But, again, let's start with history.

How It All Happened

A half-century ago few of us had health insurance, and up until the 1960s those who did, usually had coverage only for hospital stays. Starting in the 1960s employers came to be expected to provide this modern necessity, splitting the cost with their employees. This system worked well enough for most people, even those employed by small firms, until the point where medical costs broke loose from the few restraints existing. As costs went up insurance companies became both more selective and raised premiums. As premiums went up, fewer small firms and fewer individuals were able to pay. This has steadily continued to the point where it is now obvious that, unless otherwise forced to, insurers will soon accept only those in perfect health and then only up until their first illness. As mentioned, the majority of us have for a long time wanted some form of universal health insurance. Our wishes have been manifest in polls, surveys, consumer and civic activities, and proposed legislation. But, just as in handgun control, our entreaties have been ignored. The closest we came to universal health care was in 1965 during the Johnson administration. As always though, the powerful lobbying of organized medicine succeeded in defeating the threat to its pocketbook, this time with the strategy of giving in to Medicare for the elderly and Medicaid for the poor.

Medicaid is a federal and state program that was established to cover those below the poverty line and unable to pay for health care. Currently, however, Medicaid covers only 38 percent of the nation's poor, owing to raised government definition of the poverty line.

Medicare is a government program that provides medical care for those over sixty-five and which utilizes Blue Cross and Blue Shield services for paying claims.

Blue Cross and Blue Shield were founded by organized medicine in the 1930s in an attempt to provide health insurance to a greater number of people and ensure that hospitals and doctors were paid. Enjoying the tax benefits of a non-profit organization, the Blues were able to virtually monopolize the health insurance field and command large hospital discounts. This went on until the 1960s. Commercial insurers then started wooing the best risks away from Blue Cross and Blue Shield with lower premiums, leaving the worst risks for the Blues and the state-run high-risk pools. Naturally Blue Cross and Blue Shield premiums also went up, further worsening the situation. By 1990 only 22 of 74 Blue Cross and Blue Shield companies still made policies available to everyone, and most have now changed over to doing business in the same manner as other insurance carriers.[3]

In the 1970s there were a few skirmishes with those seeking universal health care, but organized medicine was again able to fight off attempts to satisfy the will of the majority. This they did by simply "paying" contributions to congressional representatives who in turn promoted the view of national health insurance as "socialized medicine".

All of this has occurred in full public view, the AMA being one of the largest contributors to political campaigns, appearing every year at or near the top of the list. For example, in 1988 the association spent $5.3 million on the congressional elections.[4] Over the years it has given its money to hundreds of congressional representatives, including two thirds of the congressional members of the Pepper Commission—a bipartisan group established to study the health care issue and recommend changes.

The AMA's perennial national spending is supplemented with additional contributions by state medical associations, also to the tune of millions of dollars. This spending is, in turn, joined by the equally generous contributions of the insurance industry, with many of the large insurance companies appearing among the top fifty contributors. The investments by the medical associations and the insurance industry have been large, but the results have been worth every cent.

It is a remarkable financial success story, for which we the public deserve major credit. For years we accepted the fiction that the only alternative to our existing system was "socialized medicine", where, granted, even more waste occurs, and the freedom of personal choice is yanked away. Of course, the AMA, insurance companies, and more recently, Health Care Cost Management Firms, played perfectly on these fears. They succeeded, for example, with their innuendos of socialized medicine, in camouflaging the true nature of the Canadian system and discrediting it in the minds of many of us. But, again, the real credit is ours for without our determination to be entertained rather than informed, there would be no target for the PR and the emotional and misleading advertising, and hence no means of perpetuating the scheme.

Today's Decision

Many of us chafe against the notion of paying for universal health care; we are understandably leery of additional and unbearable tax burdens. On the other hand, we somehow think it less evil to shell out $2,000, $3,000, or more, in yearly premiums for hole-ridden insurance policies. In both cases we pay; the object is really to get the most for our money. Anyone believing the present system provides this, or can be modified to do so, is simply unwilling to face facts.

In reality, of course, there are several alternatives open to us to organize U.S. health care. Before discussing any of them, though, we must first decide whether we wish to make health care universally available to all, or whether we agree with a former AMA president who declared that health care is a *privilege* not a right.[5] Enough polls have shown for a long time that over 60 percent of us do *not* agree with this statement, but that has not prevented the AMA from prevailing. They are, however, at least in retreat.

As in the issue of handgun control, the real question is whether we can break the campaign-fund strings which tie our fate to the wishes of the wealthiest special interest groups.

The Causes

There is no doubt that the killer cause of our health-care fiasco has been skyrocketing costs. But even without these out-of-control costs, our *system* of providing health care simply does not work. It only works well for those employed by large firms; but the self-employed, unemployed, early retirees, part-timers, divorced, and those working for small firms or even between jobs, are not so lucky. We therefore have a *total health care* problem to solve, but without immediate containment of our runaway medical costs we will soon have no chance at all for providing adequate health care, regardless of the system.

Runaway Costs: A Nightmare Come True

Since we already know the major cost contributors, the oft-used procrastination "wait until all the data is in" won't fly this time. One significant cost factor has been the overload of the system with a substantial quantity of self-inflicted ills, such as drug addiction, alcoholism, smoking addiction, craze for fire-arm violence, and willful obesity. Another has been the widespread redundancy in administration and technology. But another cause, largely and purposely unaddressed by our law makers, has been the insidious actions of our legal profession. It is here that we can take quick action towards correcting the total situation.

Our Infamous Legal Profession

As we know, medical care was not always out of reach of so many, and costs were not always spiraling upward so quickly. Over the last thirty years one group in particular has played a special role in bringing this about. Lawyers have managed to create an instant wealth builder (complementing some of their steady cash cows such as probate) by combining contingency fees and astronomical liability suits. The "astronomical" part is our doing. For it is we, the public, who as jurors, have awarded these enormous sums, of which lawyers get a tremendous cut. For every multimillion dollar suit awarded to some plaintiff by our robin-hood jurors, another law firm racks up 33, 40, or 50 percent of it.

Judges and lawyers love to praise the public (while winking at each other) as "the cornerstone of our justice system". In truth, we are also the cornerstone of what is wrong with our judicial system. The legal profession has us to thank for these huge windfalls. We have been obligingly magnanimous, awarding enormous amounts because, as far as we jurors could see, those big ol' rich insurance companies were the ones paying. There has been no rhyme or reason to these multimillion dollar awards except the obvious use of legal precedent. As soon as one jury grabbed a figure out of the air it was used as basis for an even larger settlement elsewhere, and so on. We were unable to think further and envision the predictable reaction by insurance companies to the pilfering of their coffers— raising premiums.

The contingency fee is simply an open invitation for lawyers to get rich at the expense of us all, which they have gleefully done. With this wealth they've become the aristocrats of American society. They, better than any of us, can take it easy and enter politics for the sport of it. Unfortunately for us, the legal profession is also in a great position to block any attempt at reform of their enrichment processes. They dominate our national legislature with over 45 percent of their members in congress (60 out of 100 in the Senate and 182 out of 435 in The House), and who knows how heavily they occupy state legislatures and city councilmen positions. And guess who was the number two PAC contributor last year? —none other than the *Association of Trial Lawyers*.[6]

Administration

Right now the conglomerate of private insurance carriers spend 10 to 11 percent of each health-care dollar on administration. That's roughly 66 billion dollars. Compare this with the Canadian system where only 1 to 2.5 percent is spent on administration.

The problem is compounded by the numerous schemes involved such as deductibles, coinsurance, user fees, and out-of-pocket expenses. This alone adds a substantial amount of record keeping, in order to determine payments, and creates wasteful record duplication.

Redundant Technology

High-technology equipment often winds up in several hospitals in the same community, competing with each other for patients. The result is pressure to prescribe unnecessary procedures in order to pay for the equipment.

Hospital/Doctors Fees

Average daily room charges went from $127 in 1980 to over $800 in 1990—that's over a 525 percent increase in ten years![7] (Note the excess funds available to some hospitals to buy TV and radio advertising.) The cost of medical care is increasing two to three times faster than the rate of inflation and is responsible for *two-thirds* of the large yearly increase in premiums.

Preventive Medicine: The Costly Neglect

We are also amazingly unwise in neglecting preventive medicine. Immense pain, suffering, and *costs* could be avoided if we were to spend just a fraction of our enormous $665 billion medical outlay on preventive care. Other countries, The Netherlands is a good example, recognized early on that by ensuring the health of newborns and children, a multitude of future problems and costs could be avoided. We, however, seem to view preventive medicine in the same vein as socialized medicine. In our system, mothers go without pre-natal care and check-ups go by the wayside. They are well beyond the budget of millions, even those with insurance.

Unfortunately, we seem to place health care for children into the same bin as support to unwed mothers, fearing that promoting the former will encourage welfare dependency. This is a grave mistake. To the contrary, caring for the young is one way to halt the repetitive cycle of government assistance, and thereby reduce future welfare rolls.

There was a time, in the depression of the thirties, when we could not guarantee adequate nutrition to any, much less the young. But we passed out of this stage as a nation long ago and began feeding the multitudes of other nations. The natural question that arises is too obvious to even ask.

Dereliction: Waning Sympathy

Before leaving the causes contributing to our health care plight we should also address the additional burdens placed on the system, from sources other than the natural occurrences of unavoidable accidents and illness. As we all know, a large part of our medical care problems are self-inflicted and therefore avoidable. Firearm injuries alone cost an estimated annual $429 million, just in hospital charges, and taxpayers foot the bill for over 85 percent of these charges.[8] If ambulance, doctor, and rehabilitation costs are added, the amount would be over one billion dollars!

Understandably, the majority of Americans, not drug or alcohol addicted, inflicted with aids, giving birth to crack-addicted babies, or excessively smoking or eating, feel that those who are, must bear much of the responsibility themselves. Our health care costs are therefore closely related to other social problems and will consequently benefit from their resolution.

The Cure

We now know the seriousness of our health care situation and how we got here. It's also publicly acknowledged, even by the AMA and its friends, that something is definitely wrong with our basic manner of providing health care. The figure of thirty-seven million uninsured, in itself, is proof of that.

It's also slowly sinking in that given today's medical costs a major illness, even with medical insurance, can wipe out a family's resources in one blow. In 1990 about $50,000 in medical expenses would likely be incurred for a serious heart attack. Sometimes as little as 44 percent of that amount would be covered by "major medical" insurance.

Even for those not hit by illness the situation is close to intolerable. Families with health insurance spend on the average 12 percent of their income for it, sometimes over 14 percent. Of the total amount we spend on medical care, 29 percent is paid by individual patients, compared to 31 percent by the insurance companies.[9] The rest is footed by us as taxpayers and only when we are totally poverty stricken are we eligible ourselves for Medicaid. And, of course, there's the subtle drag put on the economy when many, out of fear of losing insurance, are discouraged from moving to other jobs.

Most ironic of all, we, the taxpayers, are paying for health care for the elderly, for the very poor, for criminals, and for self-abusers, but cannot afford it for ourselves.

First A Philosophy

Now the crucial question: what to do? A first step could be to reach a consensus on principles or philosophy. Do we consider health care essential for everyone? Do we consider it a right comparable to the right to life and the right to the pursuit of happiness? Is it synonymous with these rights, or somewhere in between, or is the AMA correct in saying it's not a right at all but a privilege for those willing to pay the going rate, a rate which will soon be within reach of only the very wealthy?

Obviously, the majority of us do not consider it a privilege, deserved only by those "earning" it by becoming successful business men, or, more appropriate to our society, rock stars, movie entertainers, TV entertainers, sports entertainers, doctors, or lawyers. No, most of us think we also have claim to the medicine of today to ease our pain or keep us alive. And if we guarantee it to the elderly, the impoverished and even criminals, shouldn't we also guarantee it for ourselves? Logic would say it's about time, and a good beginning would be to state clearly our goals for health care. The following are submitted as a start:

1) Provide a level of health care that will, from early age, promote good health.
2) Provide this for everyone at a cost that is affordable.
3) Provide incentives for people to be discerning in the manner they use and pay for medical service.

First Steps

Although we probably won't get it right all at once we must, and can, take some steps right away. For example, we can gain immediate relief by putting a cap on awards in mal-practice suits. This would instantly remove one of the greatest pressures driving up premiums. Mal-practice insurance sometimes cost a hundred dollars a day and, of course, is passed on to the patient. Worse, it drives up costs even more by forcing doctors to lay on unnecessary tests merely for legal cover. Still worse, it results in unnecessary operations. One in four hospital births today are by cesarean, and the reason is all too obvious—to reduce the risks of malpractice suits.

(California recognized all this seventeen years ago but only after the AMA squared off against the ABA.) One could even argue that such caps should be made retroactive and demand that law firms cough up past windfalls into an emergency medical aid fund.
We can start immediately reducing future costs by making preventive medicine our highest priority. No matter what else we do, adequate funds should be made available. It would be impossible to make a mistake by doing this; we would not only reap immediate improved health but huge savings in future treatment costs.

Debate

Of course, if we continue today's level of debate, dominated by the same unchallenged arguments coming from those with vested interests, there can be no hope of ever solving the problem. Instead of getting better it could get worse. Currently, the persons discussing the matter in the media are predominately from special-interest groups, such as the AFL-CIO, AMA, Health Insurance Association of America, representatives of large corporations, and the like. These groups are not capable of or willing to attack the problem objectively. Their interests are singular and their effects disruptive. Take, for example, a spokesperson for a national employers association professing how much employers wished to still be involved in providing health care for their employees. Why? Why should employers wish more, not less, responsibility for the personal affairs of their employees? (Of course it gives large companies a nice edge in hiring qualified people.) It's self-serving nonsense like this that keeps us going in circles.
We must own up to the fact that our process of tying health care to private insurance, mainly through employers, has helped *lead* to this disaster. The system has only worked well for major employers and their employees—the larger employers getting the cheaper group rates—while working against the very business ethics and ideals we so often claim.

It's not only the unemployed who are penalized and left out under the present system, it's also the self-employed and the small struggling enterprises, too small or under capitalized to afford adequate health insurance. Tying health care costs to the accounting strings of large business simply is another way of granting privileges to the status quo, the mediocre, and the unresourceful, while penalizing the venturesome and the industrious. It's also another incentive for dead wood to remain implanted in companies, doing only what is necessary to keep their positions and their benefits. Are these the ideals we want to foster?

If not, we must finally unhitch medical coverage from employer responsibility. If we consider the right to health care on par with the right to life and human dignity, then there's no way around it; we must assure it for all citizens. The challenge is to do it in the most cost-effective manner possible.

By starting with agreement on goals our debate could then proceed to the various measures open to us to achieve, or at least come nearer to, our stated goals. Our debate could hopefully proceed without the inflammatory demagoguery about socialized medicine, no choice, and so on. And, of course, only those proposals or parts of proposals helping us to achieve our goals should be adopted, while clear weaknesses in any proposal should be readily admitted, not defended to the death. In other words, progress will require constructive not *promotional* debate.

Then The Proposals

First, let's examine the circulating proposals, alternative to establishing a universal health care system.

1) Create higher deductibles to encourage use of fewer medical services.
2) Do away with state mandated benefits.
3) Design stripped-down or bare-bone insurance policies that can sell for less.

4) Institute managed health care.
5) Establish more risk pools.
6) Expand Medicare coverage.
7) Reform insurance company practices.
8) Require employers to offer coverage or pay into a fund which covers the otherwise uninsured— "play or pay".

Some of these proposals deal only with cutting costs by *reducing care* or by shifting risk and costs to government, that is, to us, the public, in order to maintain profits for themselves, the special interests. They also ignore the evidence that increased costs are *not* coming from superfluous medical visits but from actual increased costs of medical services, insurance add-on profit, redundant administration, redundant technology, and fattening of lawyers' purses.

Finally, none of these proposals encourages preventive medicine or deals with the basic question of providing health care for everyone. They are, in fact, band-aide approaches whose principal goal is to keep the existing system in place.

Rather than waste our time with these non-reforms we could make a good start by looking at health-care systems the rest of the world employs. Have no fear, we aren't obligated to copy them, but we could pick out the best features to incorporate into our own system.

Canadian System

Canada does not have socialized medicine. Socialized medicine is a form of national health care which requires doctors and hospitals to work for and draw salaries from the government, and patients are assigned to clinics. Great Britain has such a system.

Canadians are free to choose doctors and hospitals and, after twenty-five years of universal health care, physician incomes are still among the highest in Canada, four to five times that of the average industrial wage. In the U.S. doctors earn five to six times the average industrial wage.[10]

Canada maintains a fee-for-service system. Health care providers still charge fees for services, but these are not set arbitrarily. They must be negotiated each year with the government which, unlike insurance companies, has an incentive to control costs. Everyone is entitled to health care and the public pays the bills through taxes rather than insurance premiums. Doctors bill the government and are reimbursed according to the negotiated fee schedules.

Hospitals each receive an annual budget. Hospital budget increases are established from a baseline budget with increases negotiated each year for inflation, new programs, and increased hospital activity. (U.S. hospitals, as we know, simply raise their daily charges at will and pass them on to insurance companies and patients.)

Since the billing system is simplified, costs are significantly cut, and bills are paid in about thirty days. There are no complicated forms for patients to fill out and no surprise non-payments by insurance companies.

As mentioned, Canada spends less on administration and bureaucracy— 1 to 2.5 percent on every health-care dollar compared to the 10 to 11 percent spent by U.S. private insurers.[11]

The Canadian system has the additional advantage, being available to everyone, of eliminating the need for medical payment coverage under workmen's compensation insurance, or automobile insurance policies, or for the liability portion of homeowner's insurance for injury claims. Most important of all, it provides its citizens with preventive medicine, especially for pregnant women.

The comparable total tax bill for a Canadian, including total health care, is significantly less than the tax bill plus health insurance plus out-of-pocket costs for his American counterpart. For example, a resident of Ontario earning $26,000 would pay total taxes of about $7,185. Approximately 19 percent of that goes toward funding health care. His U.S. counterpart would pay approximately $6,000 in federal and state taxes and another $1,950 in Social Security taxes and has funded no health care except Medicare.[12] He (or his employer) must still pay an additional $1,500 to $2,000 for health insurance plus out-of-pocket expenses and even coinsurance amounts.

There are, of course, recognized defects in the Canadian system. Although it cost 27 percent less than the U.S. system, Canada's is still the second most expensive health care system in world. But even this is not an apples to apples comparison since the Canadian system provides health care to *all* of its citizens. In addition to its high cost, the system is slow to introduce new technology (which some see actually as an advantage). There is also obvious dissatisfaction by some, but no one can expect to please everyone. It is, of course, important to determine the extent and accuracy of the reported horror stories of patients waiting unacceptable long periods for care. It is far from wise, however, to be scared off by the standard Reader's Digest article, always written by an M.D.

Finally, health care debate in Canada is far ahead of us. There is no doubt about providing universal health care for their citizens; the debate centers on practices and procedures and ways to control costs and, since everyone has the same buying power, there is no need for doctors and organized medicine to focus on anything other than patients and their needs.

The German and Dutch Systems

The German system was forced upon the Dutch during occupation in the second world war. After the war the Dutch decided to keep it. The underlining principle under both systems is "obligation", and all participants in the health care system are expected to live up to their obligations. Physicians and hospitals are required to provide necessary health care to all patients. Accent is put on "necessary" as opposed to "demanded" services, leaving this decision in large part up to health care providers. The patient is obligated to pay for services, and employers and the state are obligated to help patients pay for health care. The latter obligations are fulfilled by the mandatory purchase of health insurance, paid for, usually equally, by the employer and employee. Fees and budgets are set via national and regional negotiations between representatives of the insurers and providers. High-income employees are permitted to purchase private health insurance. In practice, however, private insurance serves to drive up the cost of care since providers are then permitted to charge higher rates than those set by negotiations, which they do with enthusiasm. Perhaps the largest problem of the system is the tendency of patients to use it frivolously, since it is available and already paid for, and virtually no out-of-pocket expense are required.

It's Time To Act

We are late, very late, in establishing universal health care for ourselves; we and South Africa are the only ones left among the industrialized nations, who have not yet addressed the matter. The situation is not without a plus side, though. We are positioned to benefit from all that has gone before us, and plenty is already known about the other health-care systems in the world, and the results being produced.

As a starting point, it would no doubt be prudent to study, for possible adoption, the policies and activities of those nations with the lowest figures in infant mortality, heart disease occurrences, and so on. Of course, countries differ in their mentalities and infrastructures, but that is no tenable argument against making use of their experiences. It is also true that many health benefits result from activities outside of health care, such as good dietary habits, careful waste disposal, pollution control, and so on. We cannot afford to overlook these fundamentals either.

On the other hand, our situation can only become worse the longer we delay and the farther we chase the red herring of "socialized medicine". For decades we've allowed others to misinform us, and there is no reason to hope that those perpetrating this situation are suddenly going to recede by themselves. Equally disastrous would be to allow ourselves to be continually placated by the empty action of appointing a "presidential commission" in order to *appear* to be dealing with the problem, before heading on out to the golf course.

Genuine health care reform will not come unaided via our political system, not as long as we allow, or rather force, politicians to chase campaign contributions from special-interest groups under a system of indirect bribery. By continuing to condone current practices—political commercials, large monetary contributions, and our own lethargy—we will assure the success of special-interest groups, such as the AMA and insurance industry, in steadfastly thwarting genuine health care reform, using their enormous wealth, not to better explain their positions, as they will maintain, but to get legislators to block unwanted legislation.

Chapter 6

Governing Ourselves

A Beautiful Design

The accolade of course refers to our Constitution—its original seven articles and subsequent twenty-six amendments. As we know, it establishes a three-branch body for governing, consisting of the legislative, the judicial, and the executive. Checks and balances are cleverly placed on each branch, and distinct rules are proscribed. In addition, it declares certain federal, state, and individual rights, which are not to be violated. It confers power on citizens to directly elect their legislative representatives and indirectly elect the head of the executive branch—election of the president is actually a process whereby voters choose electors who are each pledged to cast their vote for their party's candidate on the first Monday after the second

Wednesday in December—who has the right to appoint, subject to approval by the Senate, the heads of the third branch, the Supreme Court justices.

The design is straight forward, only a dozen or so pages long. It's durable, flexible, and has been tested for over two hundred years. It *must* be sound. Nonetheless, there is *one* slight flaw: an assumption is made about the population. It's a reasonable assumption so there shouldn't be any problem. Nevertheless, if the assumption ever becomes untrue the entire design collapses. The founding fathers assumed the *majority* of citizens would be able to weigh issues and decide collectively who or what best represented their interests. Presumably, if they couldn't do this there was no justification for self-government anyway.

Not that voters were expected to devote long hours in following each and every issue. After all, they would need to make a living and also have time left to relax and rejuvenate themselves. The only actual requirement was that they have enough interest to keep themselves reasonably well informed. Failing that, they were expected to at least be willing and able to listen to an exposition of facts, arguments, and counter arguments and come to a reasonable conclusion. (In their defense, our founding fathers had no way of foreseeing television, especially deregulated, free-wheeling commercial television.)

The design seems sound. The flaw appears minor, the assumption being a reasonable one. We must conclude the system is a good one. So what's the problem? Why has our only vehicle for change and problem resolution suddenly broken down?

The Times They Are Here (Murphy's Arrival)

True to Murphy's law if anything can possibly go wrong, it will. We have stumbled into the one pitfall impeding our way, and other nations are blindly following. It's obviously an innate human defect that as prosperity increases and more and more entertainment is available and affordable, more and more is consumed. The more time spent in entertainment the less time available for absorbing real information. Emotion gradually replaces reason. Eventually, with continued prosperity, the point is reached where the voting majority can no longer govern themselves, for lack of the bare essentials.

In the U.S. we have already reached this point or at least are dangerously near it. We see deterioration all around us, but we are befuddled as to why. We continue praising the system and ourselves, and continue talking about *getting out the vote and returning power to the people*. But we the people are exactly the problem. We are not informed enough to even serve as an audience for reasoned discussion.

Meanwhile, our democratic system continues functioning as designed, simply adjusting itself to an under-educated and over-entertained public, while still embodying our cherished principles. For example, we have always held that individuals are and should be motivated by personal gain. It's the foundation of our economic system and drives us in practically all other matters. We must therefore expect the same principle to direct the actions of our elected representatives.

In theory, of course, their personal gain is directly connected to ours. If they fail to properly represent our interests, which are sometimes narrow (retaining local environmentally damaging jobs) but often wider (reducing the runaway budget deficit), then—wham—they are out. We will elect someone else.

That's the theory anyway, and it should work. Yet it only works when voters actually *know* what is in their interest and can judge critically the events that are unfolding in front of their eyes. Without this type of voter the game becomes a different one. Much more important than taking reasoned and rational actions, which represent our interests, is simply to give the impression of doing so. Image becomes all important, much more than substance, and image making is the business of television. The interests of voter and elected representative are no longer directly complementary.

Politicians are dealing with a new breed of voter today and they know it. We, the humongous mass of uninformed voters are all suffering from mental malnutrition. Virtually all information we get is ingested intravenously through the TV tube we're connected to every day for about five or six hours. Any doses of real information must first be dissolved in lots of accompanying entertainment, otherwise we refuse it. News, for example, must begin or end with entertaining chatter and be delivered by a commentator who signals with eyebrow or voice inflection so we know how to feel about what we've just seen and heard.

We do, of course, have editorials and a few exceptional programs like Face the Nation or Meet the Press which elicit real discussion, but they are watched only by the minority. Commercials are what get *our* attention, appeals to the emotion, not some dry discussions. We, the majority, millions and millions of us, are the determinants of this democracy, and if you want our votes you better not bore us with facts and discussion. And you better not take too much time away from our entertainment either, thirty seconds max. That's the longest we can pay attention to something that's not entertaining.

Listen to the words of a successful candidate: "My frustration is we have to be convincing in our argument but we can't go too far because you put'em to sleep. The American people want to watch TV, and if you can get your message in just after the movie and before the commercial, you've reached their minds...."[1]

And of course, with only fifteen or thirty seconds, and an audience which has no background knowledge to rely on, negative TV commercials are even better politics. A recognized expert was Bush campaign manager Lee Atwater who explained his simple but successful formula: "You have to make the case that the other guy, the other candidate, is a bad guy."[2]

So here we are, attempting to practice democracy with little in our heads but entertainment and yet hoping and believing that somehow all problems will be taken care of. Only by a war, by our own unemployment, or by an election (also made as entertaining as possible) are we ever really distracted from our amusements. Now we're ready to uncover just who is to blame and which candidate is our shining knight and which is a losing wimp. We're ready to vote! To this day we've avoided facing the reality that we, the public, are the problem. Some have suspected, others have seen it clearly, but no one wants to come out and say it openly. It would be tantamount to admitting that we as a people are pretty much useless in governing ourselves. No one wants to risk being the messenger who delivers such unflattering and unwelcome news.

Elections Gone Haywire

The democratic institution most obviously damaged by our own neglect is our election process. It's now a farce. Granted, some may be having town meetings, or otherwise following a rational process, in a few isolated pockets around the country. But they fade to insignificance when compared to the big picture. TV commercials overwhelmingly determine our elections. And many of us don't even get it. Surprisingly, Jim Lehrer of McNeil/Lehrer Newshour still had not apparently realized this when he asked Paul Tsongas in astonishment "Wait a minute. Are you saying that TV commercials are defining American elections?" Tsongas had just finished explaining that he was dropping out of the primaries because he had no money with which to buy TV commercials in the upcoming New York primary, and therefore had no chance at all.

Politicians know all this. They realize they must get the attention of us, the know-nothing multimillions, before the ugly competition does, and the best time for that is when we're gawking at the tube. Candidates and incumbents cannot afford to give much attention to what *informed* people think about issues. That's not how elections are won or lost. It's the masses that count, our general likes and dislikes. And our emotional hot buttons are well known. We don't like taxes nor do we like moral complications in our leaders. We like flags, movie and sports heroes, and to be told that God loves and favors us the most.

Knowing this, no political candidate in his right mind would try to run a major campaign without a public relations expert to line up and produce his commercials, that is, create his image. For elections we call these image makers campaign managers and their chief expertise is media science, not political science. "Image is everything!", as one popular TV commercial blatantly proclaims.

The Washington Post knows all this too. In a front page article on the resignation of Ross Perot's campaign manager and Perot's subsequent withdrawal, they proclaimed with astonishment: "The world may never know, exactly, what Perot thought he was getting. Perhaps he envisioned a dull, high-minded campaign in which he would patiently explain the issues to America."[3] Heaven forbid! We would all look down upon such an unexciting campaign. Most probably, the Washington Post would not even cover it.

Political incumbents and aspirants, knowing the game, also know they need money, lots of money. Without it they're dead in the water. Whoever has the most can afford the best copywriters and the most effectual commercials, as well as other forms of advertising, and therefore will win the most votes. It's straight business arithmetic. Obtaining public office is a commercial enterprise, and political commercials are expensive, competing for the same TV slots needed by our largest companies to sell beer, cars, and deodorant.

The result of this cycle of hustling for campaign money, to purchase TV commercials, to determine election outcome, is no longer democracy; it is government chosen and conducted à la the free-market system. Instead of a democratic form of government and a free-market economy we have a free-market government and a neglected, out-of-control, economy.

TV commercials even prod us to "get out and vote". They *never* prod us to get up, get informed, and turn off the damn TV. If they did there would be no more audience for emotion-arousing commercials, no audience for the "sunset in the background scenes" or the tortured strands of background music. Goods and services would have to be offered based on boring things such as value and quality. The whole economy, as it's now constructed, would collapse.

This calamitous situation also leaves elected officials with little time left to spend on issues. Congressional voting is seldom held on Mondays or Monday evenings because that day is set aside for fundraising activities. Fridays are out too, as congressmen and congresswomen rush to catch planes back home for local fund-raising activities.

There is a connecting thread, of course, running through our neglect in education, our addiction to entertainment, and this disastrous election process based on public ignorance. On the positive side, it's also clear that reversing our attitude towards education will also directly and beneficially affect the other two.

The Way Back

Unfortunately there's no short cut back to a functioning democracy. Education takes time. We will not become educated overnight and definitely not with docudrama and newsmagazine shows. Nor does it help to dress up issues in the drama of a court room setting, such as the recent attempt on Public Television to broach the subject of education in America. If we are not mature enough to pay attention and accept information without an accompanying entertaining twist, it's hardly likely we can be of any help in resolving anything.

Either we master television, or it will master us. It is *the* communication medium which gets to us all; we can't change that. We can, however, begin to use it wisely, not inanely for our own self-destruction. For example, we could and should insist on the strict separation of news and documentary information from entertainment. If we continue to be unwilling to do this, we should simply kiss our common future good-bye, for there can be no doubt, at the present rate, we will rapidly stupefy ourselves into oblivion.

But returning to our malfunctioning democracy, there is one small but rational step which, by itself, promises to reverse the deterioration. Imagine, if we were to emphasize the *responsibility* of a vote, instead of merely its performance. Certainly, a vote based solely on uninformed reaction to emotional stimuli is worse than no vote at all, and rather than encourage each other to get out and vote, we would be wiser to encourage each other to first become informed. In fact, we would be better off if only 1 percent of our population went to the polls, if those 2,500,000 were informed. All of our superficial campaigns, as well as the corruptive influence of its spending, would disappear overnight, and we would finally have a solid process again, based on that rare quantity, genuine emotion-free information.

Ban Political Advertising

Since the majority of us are manipulated by it, rely on it instead of informing ourselves, we have no choice but to prohibit it. It does not inform; more often it misinforms. As in war time we must protect our soldier voters from this enemy propaganda. Political commercials contribute absolutely nothing to the democratic process, not even, as some would argue, in the role of providing summary information.

Even posters and bill-boards with names, faces, and slogans are out of place. These should announce an upcoming election, not a candidate's name. What good is merely a name and a slogan, except to the pitiable voter entering the voting booth in the same state of mind he approaches a confusing supermarket buying decision, looking for a familiar brand name? Could this be the explanation for name banners and placards appearing just before the voting polls? Are they there for the poor lost soul who otherwise hasn't a clue on how to vote? Or are they there to assure him that he his "jumping on the bandwagon"?

Chapter 6 - Governing Ourselves 103

We must admit, many of our current practices have little to do with democracy. We simply kid ourselves into believing they do. Party conventions, for example, are basically insider events, leaving the rest of us to simply gawk at the hoopla. But, by far, the most inane development of all, and the one presenting the greatest immediate threat to democracy, is the TV political commercial.

Ideally, we should simply raise a population which would consider TV political commercials an insult to their intelligence, and would, as well, expect and demand informative nightly news, not staged concern from anchor newspersons, who are paid the same multimillions as the rest of our entertainers. In the meantime, however, we can at least acknowledge the emergency and take some urgent steps to defend ourselves from the exploitation.

Already, there are signs that we have reached the point where we cannot even recognize manipulation when it is placed squarely in front of our eyes. A large part of our election commentary and analysis, for example, is *about* TV ads. "Candidate so-and-so ran 50 separate ads in six weeks." "Some 150 ads per day were shown, sometimes six or seven in a row."[4] We treat this as part of the legitimate election process when, in effect, we are watching and discussing someone buying his way into leadership of us all—BY BUYING UP TV ADS! Could anything be more ludicrous than elections based on advertising fluff?

Given our reaction to past threats, however, the most we can probably expect is forced appendage to the commercials of the now standard public admonition: "WARNING: This political candidate, if elected, may be dangerous to your health and welfare. He may cause such side effects as nausea, loss of appetite, vomiting, hypertension, high blood pressure, palpitations, severe headaches, and nervousness."

Minimize Campaign Contributions

One possible and feasible back-door means of eliminating political TV and radio commercials would be to limit campaign contributions, from corporations and individuals alike, to an absolute minimum, say the Jerry Brown $100. Available funds would then unlikely be sufficient to purchase these deadly effective commercials.

Another approach could be equally effective. If national TV and radio time for candidates were to be offered *only* via the public airways, and *only* for debate, there would be no target for spending the large contributions, at least nothing so directly effective.

Either way, we will have taken a step forward.

Debate Publicly

Ideally, at election time, public television and radio should be used to present candidates and their ideas by way of in-depth discussions, not the prime-time "show" events of old, and arranged in a forum, such as Public Television recently introduced, whereby competent moderators probe the candidates for real substance on real issues. These could be a series of four or more debates, say, two hours each.

In these debates/discussions irrelevancies and evasions would be discouraged. There is no reason why candidates, who are unwilling or unable to answer a question, should be permitted to disguise this. Today's politician knows not to answer questions which risk disadvantage. Instead, he or she employs *motherhood* or pat standbys— speech which merely contains good sounding, but hollow, words and phrases, usually beginning as follows:

Chapter 6 - Governing Ourselves 105

The American people expect ...
This great nation of ours will ...
We're still the greatest nation in the world ...

Haynes Johnson, author of *Sleepwalking Through History* said it well: "America's presidential election process is also too long, too costly, and too driven by public opinion polls and advertising tactics." The situation will worsen, he says, until the political parties agree "to hold a series of true nationally televised debates for their presidential candidates...."

With TV and radio commercials banned, political candidates would be left only with the traditional means of campaigning. The voter could inform himself via these debates and discussions, or by following the daily accounts of the candidates' speeches and comments. Should he choose not to inform himself, he would have no basis for voting. There would be no TV or radio commercials to implant pseudo information in his head. Neither would there be a poster to save him from total embarrassment upon entering the voting booth. The mindless vote would finally be discouraged!

Honest debate, rather than prepared speeches, is also absolutely necessary if we are ever to resolve important issues such as abortion and health care insurance. Needed is information, not orchestrated propaganda. Public discussions should be *exchanges* and speakers should be those with something to contribute, not those merely touting or defending a political line. Such informative sessions would also be helpful in guiding congressional debate in which, by the way, the president should also be expected to participate.

It's time to bring the executive office down to the working level of a prime minister and stop shielding it from everyday realities. If aloof royalty is desired, would it not be better to create a separate office, as many nations have? It is obvious that the ceremonial aspect of the executive office has been noticeably overdone by recent presidents, with some spending more time in photo opportunities, diplomatic functions, and especially personal recreation, than probably any other elected official on earth. It would be interesting to compare at least one president who comes to mind, to the average citizen, in the number of days spent pursuing golf, tennis, hunting, fishing, boating, and other fun activities.

For both the election process and our subsequent efforts to resolve national issues, we need debate. We need it to transport facts and ideas and dispose of refuse, in the same manner the body needs healthy arteries and veins to transport blood. Without the discipline of informed and sincere debate we will continue, in our current grand style, to accomplish nothing, other than perhaps adding to the global warming trend.

Demand Information

Press conferences no longer inform, at least not in the amount that they should. Do we really need, for example, the press asking ingratiating and cute questions such as "what is your mood today?" or "how did you like your broccoli?" Don't we get enough entertainment elsewhere? The entire practice has become far more of a "show" event than an information disseminating process. Far better would be to replace the press by those with more vested interest, such as members of the opposition party, those of opposing views, or simply members of the public.

We need to elicit more *information* from "press" conferences or any forum where issues are discussed. Since we don't demand it, today's elected officials are experts at giving no information at all, and by now all of us have indelibly implanted in our minds the time-worn expressions:

> We're looking into this very closely.
> We're continuing to monitor the situation.
> This is a matter of great concern to ... [me and my staff, the president, the administration, the great American public, or whatever]

Let me just first say [a deluge of irrelevant things so that everybody will forget the question]

* * *

As already mentioned, democracy was obviously intended for the informed. Their views, after all, are sounder than those of the uninformed, and they have *earned* the privilege of participating. It is also fitting that those not interested enough to inform themselves on an issue or an election should live with the consequence— permitting those who do care, to direct the nation's affairs.

There would even be good argument (although impracticable) to require each voter to pass a written test, showing knowledge of the candidates and the important issues, *before* being permitted to vote. Assuming 100 percent literacy, no one could charge discrimination against anything but mental laziness or indifference. As a bonus, it would increase the demand for sources of real information. We don't permit people to drive cars before proving they understand what driving is about. Shouldn't we perhaps treat the practice of voting with the same prudence? After all, its careless exercise poses even more danger to us all.

It has been argued that people who don't follow the issues don't vote anyway. Unfortunately, many millions do. In the 1988 presidential election 91,594,809 of us voted. That was 45.65 percent of the eligible voting population, so a greater number indeed did not vote. It is reported, though, that less than 3 percent of us read books and less than 15 percent read newspapers. Assuming those same ratios for our 1988 voters, we had perhaps, at the most, about 16.5 million voting with some knowledge. This means that the other 75 million voted on the basis of TV commercials or for equally frivolous reasons.

We can, in fact, compare ourselves to the fledgling and teetering democracy of Kenya, where television, radio, and word of mouth are the *only* means of information available to the majority, and of course, the object of desired control by competing forces. The singular difference is that in Kenya the majority *cannot* read newspapers or books; in the U.S. the majority either cannot or *will not* read newspapers or books.

Of course, requiring a demonstration of fitness to vote is not feasible, and our assumption of 100 percent literacy is far from being achieved, not to mention the many who would find it threatening to their conception of democracy. The best we can do, therefore, is to encourage the informed, while discouraging the uninformed vote. And, as mentioned, prohibiting political commercials would go a long way towards encouraging the genuine informing process, as would focusing discussions and debates on Public Television. We can perhaps never overcome the fact that human nature inclines towards apathy, until aroused by matters of immediate personal concern, but we can at least be wise enough to remove the effects of this habitual apathy as far away as possible from our governing process.

Vote Smart

At the moment it is, of course, difficult to do so. The media continues to feed us the fluff we have so long showed to be our chief interest, and without a change in our attitudes, we can hardly expect their sudden about-face and willful economic suicide. We, the public, must take the first action. One group has.

In Oregon an information system using a computer data bank and an 800 number has been set up to provide voters with substantive information. That information consists of how the candidates voted on various issues in the past, their position on current issues, their stated goals and priorities, and so on.

Its number as of this writing is:

1-800-786-6885

Its managers intend it to be a starting point "where people can do an end run around all of the manipulative nonsense". They hope to reconnect voters with factual information "absolutely crucial to their struggle to self-government."
Its director is former Arizona politician Richard Kimball who ran unsuccessfully for the U.S. Senate in 1986. He recounts that his moment of illumination came when he was offered a $50,000 campaign contribution from the AFL-CIO. The first $20,000 was to be spent for a pollster to determine his most positive attribute, which turned out to be his birth in the state. The remaining $30,000 was then earmarked for an emotional commercial playing up his roots. He was shown feeding carrots to horses in the Arizona sunset near the grand canyon and picking off fruit from Arizona orange trees "with a sunset literally, at the end of the commercial, behind my head". It was that experience which made Richard Kimball realize how shallow and superficial the entire process had become.
As might be expected one third of the candidates, mostly incumbents, want no part of this factual source of information. With 435 congressional, 35 Senate, and 12 governor seats open in the 1992 election, as well as the presidency, a total of up to 1,000 candidates are expected. *Vote Smart* anticipates from experience, however, that more than 300 will refuse to be interviewed.[5]

The Power Of Individual Action

In addition to *Vote Smart* there is other good news. The system, which has served us so well in the past, is still sound. It will work beautifully for an informed, educated and interested people. We can even thank the NRA and other special interest groups for demonstrating some of its built-in strengths.
For example, letter writing to elected representatives is still a powerful and highly desirable instrument of influence. Even those below the voting age can wield it.

Politicians have clearly demonstrated that they are moved by a significant outpouring of mail on any subject. First, they realize that people taking the trouble to write will probably take the time to vote and, if they fail to respond properly, maybe not for them. Second, they cannot help surmising that for every letter written there are many more voters who feel the same way. Finally, anytime mail piles up on any issue it gets the attention of the press and thereby multiplies in its impact.

It is also clear that, with public apathy currently the norm, any sudden show of public excitement gets the immediate attention of elected officials. A good example occurred during the aftermath of Desert Storm. Everyone felt extreme relief when the war was over, especially president George Bush, since he obviously saw the result as a boon for his reelection chances, and could hardly wait to arrange a victory parade. One nagging problem, however, was the tragic and mass exodus of Kurdish men, women, and children, fleeing for their lives into the icy mountains with nothing but the clothes on their backs.

The situation obviously called for U.S. presidential leadership, especially since George Bush had encouraged their uprising all along. Two simple no-risk actions could have been taken: (1) order the grounding of all Iraqi helicopters and (2) order the routing of humanitarian relief directly to non-Iraqi-government entities.

As we all know, however, no presidential leadership emerged, absolutely none. George Bush was back on the golf course from where he was forced to field a few questions from the press. Because journalists continued to press the matter and keep the tragedy in the public eye, the president was finally forced to defend his inaction with weak remarks to the effect that the American people were not writing or voicing any concern to him. Only the journalistic world, as far as he was concerned, was trumpeting for action.

Suddenly, there was a deluge of calls and letters directed at the white house. People had been clearly told what they had to do to make this president act. Within twenty-four hours the administration reversed itself and contradicted its previous rhetoric. It was too late for thousands of innocent, helpless Kurdish and Shiite women and children, but it shows that letter writing does work and that the individual can wield political power, if he or she is willing to make the effort.

Chapter 7

Education of Another Kind

We arrive at last at the core of both our failure and our hope. As H.G. Wells aptly put it: future human existence is "a race between education and catastrophe." That being the case, it's time for us to hurry to the starting blocks.

Democracies are mushrooming everywhere, authoritarian rule is on the wane, and there has probably never been a more opportune moment in history to abolish rule by force and establish global rule by reason. As more democracies take root, however, the more important becomes the individual voter and the less important the individual statesman. The decisions controlling life and death now fall to the every-day citizen, the voter. No longer can Mr. and Ms. Citizen rely on a few intelligent, competent, often ruthless, people to take up the daily business of ruling. It's also highly unlikely an Alexander, or Frederick, or Catherine The Great will step forward in today's situation. The purse is too small; they can do much better duping than ruling the masses. It's now entirely up to the common citizenry to "grow its own" intelligent and competent leadership to both direct and administer the state.

But where will these leaders come from if nowhere education and understanding are being nurtured? Can they possibly emerge from a population in which "less than five percent of its seventeen-year-olds can understand literary essays, historical documents, scientific materials, and other reading matter of the type encountered in college textbooks"?[1] And even if by some miracle some competent leaders do emerge, could they be understood? Would they have any chance at election, against even the most mediocre electronic media star, in a country where "21 million adults cannot read at the fourth grade level,"[2] and, even among high-school graduates, "forty percent cannot read at the ninth-grade level"?[3] Not likely, not when there is one TV set per 1.3 persons, and the average time spent watching the tube leaves little remaining for anything else.

This double-edged challenge of pervasive entertainment and rapidly deteriorating education is far greater than all other challenges combined, for if it is not met, democracy is doomed to vote for its own destruction at the hands of its favorite charlatan. Ours will be one of the first to go. On the other hand, the smallest reversal in our disastrous approach to education and entertainment, is bound to generate immediate corrective momentum.

Notwithstanding the corrosive influence of entertainment saturation, it makes sense to concentrate on education, since only the educated person is motivated to reject mindless entertainment. If, however, we continue the farce of using entertainment as a means of education (educational games, docudrama, TV commercials) we will no doubt become a classic case for future historians—a people who, once donning the intoxicating glasses of entertainment, never looked back, leaping gleefully to their demise.

It's education or catastrophe, the choice is ours. If we do have the sense to choose education we will immediately encounter a fortunate and simple principle, a natural law, just waiting to lend us a hand. *Learning is the natural product of interest.* It is the mere process of satisfying curiosity that produces learning. To educate we need really do nothing more than support, not hinder, this natural process. If, nevertheless, we choose to ignore this truth, as well as history, we will be committing the same grievous error of communism. A dictated education, just as a dictated socioeconomic system, destroys the power, initiative, and potential of the human being.

Is interest really the secret? Can it really turn the tide? Yes and no. It is potent enough to accomplish education but not if its fervor is dulled by entertainment. So far, we have allowed entertainment, like a cancer, to insidiously crowd out healthy interest and replace it with the narcosis of make-believe—not only for ourselves but for our children. This is evident when observing young children, who's imagination, not allowed to work for itself, is limited to the images of television. But putting aside for the moment the equally threatening problem of entertainment, let us concentrate on education with the goal of unleashing its power, not because it will bring us a technological edge over the rest of the world, but simply because it is our only path to survival.

The majority of us, using ourselves as a measure, would agree that interest is at the heart of learning and that most of what we learn is actually self-acquired. Looking back we are forced to admit that most of our present knowledge came from outside of the classroom. The subjects of history and foreign languages come particularly to mind. Attempts by schools to force feed us with these subjects usually provoked aversion, not interest. Later we may have discovered easy and interesting ways to learn foreign languages, as well as the surprising truth that interesting books on history actually do exist. Will and Ariel Durant's twelve volumes of integral history, for example, contain all of the history most human beings could read in a lifetime, and one taste of their interestingly presented *Story of Civilization* can easily awaken an appetite for more. All fields of knowledge are vulnerable like this to the powerful onslaught of interest. Our public school system, however, seems expertly designed to *destroy* natural interests, and the implementation of the design has been remarkably effective.

But, before proceeding with discussions on what to do about today's educational mess, let us, as before, place ourselves on the solid ground of history. Let us review the ideas and experiments on education already expressed or tried, which have resulted in today's American educational system.

> People with no understanding of their history are lost in the present and unable to plan the future.
> —Christopher Lasch in The Culture of Narcissism

Some Facts on the History of Education

Our purpose here is not to present a full history of education but only to touch upon some major developments (in western culture) contributing to our present-day situation. Plato and Aristotle offer a good starting point. Both broached the problem of education fully realizing its importance for society's survival.

The Beginnings

Plato

In his *Republic,* Plato, speaking through Socrates, is concerned with defining justice, its worth, and its effects on the individual soul. To do so, he sets about first describing a just society and comes eventually to the question of education. In constructing the theoretically just society and its education, Plato differentiates between Rulers, Guardians, and Craftsmen, whom he sees as society's deliberative/legislative, executive, and productive bodies. He comes to many common-sense conclusions, among them that, since stories are a child's first form of education, it does no good for the poets, such as Hesiod and Homer, to concoct stories which portray the gods engaging in rage, violence, deceit, and criminal deeds, be they allegorical or not. The child, Plato points out, cannot distinguish the allegorical from the literal, and the ideas he takes in are likely to become indelibly fixed in his mind.

Plato is also concerned that citizens take up places in his theoretical society for which they are most inclined and qualified and concludes that, from the well-educated guardians of the state, the best will emerge as rulers who rule from a position of wisdom, courage, and concern for the welfare of their society and its citizens.

Although most would have trouble accepting all of Plato's positions on education, his ideas were developed from clear and rational thinking, and this thinking has continued to be relevant for some 2400 years. (He was perhaps also the first to point to a nagging problem, apparently plaguing ancient Greece as it does modern civilization: "Law and medicine begin to give themselves airs, when, even among free men, large numbers take too keen an interest in them.") His lucid thinking also extended to equal rights for women (although not for slaves, but neither did the thoughts of Jesus) and he is wholly convincing when, in discussing the burdens the guardians will encounter, states: "If a sound education has made them reasonable men, they will easily see their way through all these matters as well as others ...."

Aristotle

Plato's foremost pupil, Aristotle, demonstrating what good education can spawn, proceeded to make his own mark by laying an immense foundation for learning that continued to benefit mankind for two thousand years. After dispensing Alexander the Great's education (for four years, beginning when Alexander was age thirteen) he opened in 334 BC a school of rhetoric and philosophy, later to be called the Lyceum.

With the assistance of his pupils, Aristotle set about gathering an immense store of scientific observations in virtually every field imaginable, enough to fill an encyclopedia. More importantly, he achieved the consolidation of these new data with previously recorded information. He began by defining a clear form of definition, which consisted of specifying an object or idea by naming the genus or class to which it belonged, followed by the specific difference that distinguished it from all other members of that class. He also formulated ten aspects under which anything might be categorized (substance, quantity, quality, relation, place, time, position, possession, activity, passivity) and accepted the senses as the only source of knowledge.

In the field of logic Aristotle's treatises functioned as *the textbook of logic* for two thousand years. His use of the syllogism in deductive reasoning and his establishment of the principal of contradiction, contributed to his recognition as the father of scientific method. He argued that the heavenly bodies—certainly the earth—were spherical, pointing out that only a spherical earth could explain the shadow cast on the moon when eclipsed by the intervention of the earth between it and the sun. Aristotle offered explanations of clouds, fog, dew, frost, rain, snow, hail, wind, thunder, lighting, the rainbow, and meteors—not accepting supernatural explanations—and proceeded in this field of exploration as far as natural science could go, without the invention of further instrumentation.

It was in biology, however, where he was the most active and also made the most mistakes (he or his pupils). With the help of his band of students he gathered numerous data on the fauna and flora of the Aegean countries, bringing together the first-ever scientific collection of animals and plants. His enquiries spread over a vast and varied field, including the organs of digestion, excretion, sensation, locomotion, reproduction, and defense. He studied the varieties and activities of fishes, birds, reptiles, apes, and hundreds of other groups by researching their mating seasons, methods of bearing and rearing young, their habitats and migrations, their parasites and diseases, and their modes of sleep and hibernation.

Aristotle was particularly interested in the reproductive structures and habits of animals and anticipated many theories of nineteenth century biology. He delved into the phenomena of puberty, menstruation, conception, pregnancy, abortion, heredity, and twins. In noticing the analogous organs among animals, such as the nail and the claw, the feather and fish scale, as well as the similarities between ape and man, he even came close to a theory of evolution.

In philosophy, Aristotle maintained that the good life was the happy life, and the secret of happiness was action, which he defined as the exercise of energy in a way suited to a man's nature and circumstances. But he also held that thought was the distinguishing excellence of man and "the proper working of man is a working of the soul in accordance with reason."

On Government, Aristotle collected and studied with his students some 158 Greek constitutions. He then divided them into three types: monarchy, aristocracy, and timocracy, concluding that each form of government was good when the ruling power sought the good of all rather than its own profit.

It is easy to see that Aristotle did more to start the process of mankind's education than any other ancient figure we know. As the "first of Schoolmen" and, although guilty of many errors, he is an encouraging testimony to the elastic range of the human intellect and an inspiration to anyone who cares about the pursuit of knowledge and understanding.

The Long Sleep and Awakening

We next jump to the fall of the Roman Empire where education, firmly and solely in the hands of the church, fell to its dismal nadir. After the long night of the Dark Ages, education dawned again when Thomas Aquinas and the Renaissance revived the ancient culture of Greece and Rome, making man rather than God the focal point of learning. Leonardo da Vinci (1452-1519) drew attention again to the importance of observation and experimentation and contributed intricate anatomical studies. Francis Bacon (1561-1626) helped to popularize scientific techniques, and in the field of astronomy, discoveries by Copernicus, Kepler, Galileo, and Bruno helped lead us back towards understanding the universe. Isaac Newton and René Descartes pushed us forward in physics and mathematics. But the event that would eventually most affect colonial America was the eruption of the Protestant Reformation in the sixteenth century.

Early American Education

The Luther-led Reformation, together with the Catholic Counter-Reformation, brought about the settlement of America by those deeply engrossed in religious ideals and purposes. The Puritans, settling in New England, and the Presbyterians, Quakers, and Catholics who followed, helped found a nation where the most conservative ideas, such as the evil nature of man, were rigidly preserved. We see the consequence of this heritage still evident today in the arguments over prayer in school, as well as in the war between conservative theology and secular humanism. Resistance to any knowledge that conflicts with religious dogma still plagues us, centuries and centuries after the virulent opposition of religion to the important and enlightening discoveries of Copernicus, Galileo, and Bruno.

Education started in America as a duty of the family, but by 1642 the General Court of Massachusetts found many parents were neglecting the training of their children. In 1647 the Massachusetts court passed the Old Deluder Satan Act requiring every town to either set up a school or pay a sum of money to the next larger town for the support of education. These earliest schools taught religion, reading, and writing and followed closely the Puritan mentality, including flogging—contrived to "beat the devil out of the child". The chief learning method was subject matter memorization by the student, followed by testing in recitation sessions before the master.

As we approached the American Revolution capitalism had already provided growth and prosperity and a strong middle class. Newspapers flourished, colleges were established, and libraries abounded, with most books, however, coming from England. European influences, such as the ideas of John Locke (1632-1704) —the mind at birth is passive and like a blank tablet—as well as those of Ben Franklin (1706-1790)—promoting self-education for practical utility—began to lay the foundation for free and universal public education. John Amos Comenius (1592-1671) contributed by encouraging the publication of dictionaries, textbooks, and encyclopedias. He also strongly contended that learning comes from experience, that our sense organs are our teachers, and that education *was possible* for the populace.

European Influence Takes Hold

The period of Enlightenment, which captured Europe in the eighteenth century as a protest against both the authority of Christian dogma and that of absolute monarchs, transited the ocean. Our revolutionary leaders were aroused by both European events and the liberal and humanitarian ideas professed by Montesquieu, Rousseau, Voltaire, Hume, Kant, Dieterot, and others. This influence clearly showed itself in the post revolutionary years when figures such as Benjamin Rush, Noah Webster, Thomas Jefferson, Samuel Smith, Samuel Knox and Du Pont de Nemours pushed for a public system of education "necessary for a free and self-governing republic."

Yet progress towards this goal, as well as changes to the American curricula, occurred only gradually, as Horace Mann (1796-1859) worked with James G. Carter (1795-1845) to push for common school education in the country. Meanwhile, kindergartens, spawned by the ideas of the German educator Friedrich Froebel (1782-1852), took root here in 1856 and became a fixture in the American system.

Other Europeans who influenced with their concepts the development of U.S. education, in addition to those already mentioned, included the three *Johanns*: Johann Basedow, Johann H. Pestalozzi, and Johann Herbart.

Coming Up To Modern Times

Primary school education in the U.S. was at first not seen as a responsibility of the state, since it was customary for mothers to teach reading and writing to their children *before* sending them to school. Gradually, however, primary schools were established to take over this function, and eventually they became consolidated with grammar and writing schools to form the eight-year elementary school.

In 1821 the first American high school (the English High School in Boston) was established. Thereafter, the growth of high schools was at first slow: when the civil war began there were some 300, one third of which were in Massachusetts. After the Civil War, however, growth was accelerated, as a major principle of education was put into practice—public education should be free to all—and in Michigan the *Kalamazoo Case* established the right of the states to levy taxes for public high schools (1872). Also, about this time (1870), the still-existing National Education Association was formed.

Higher education in the U.S., that beyond high school, was also slow to develop until the Morrill Act of 1862, when almost every state proceeded to create a land-grant college. And in 1876 Johns Hopkins became our first graduate school—established to "create new knowledge and support scientific investigation rather than merely transfer information and skills."

Other milestones were reached, in 1826 when the first college degree was granted to a black student, and in 1868 when the Fourteenth Amendment gave black Americans citizenship. Nevertheless, these proved to be sterile achievements for blacks. Given the steadfast attitude of whites, Booker T. Washington, then the leading black educator, chose to concentrate on practical and vocational education. His Tuskegee Normal and Industrial Institute became the present-day model for black colleges. Minority (black) education then grew slowly up until the first world war. Next came the test for complete dominance of public education. The Oregon legislature passed a law which required all children to attend *public* schools until they reached sixteen years of age, thereby shutting out private schools. The U.S. Supreme court ruled, however, in 1925 that, although the state had a right to inspect and regulate private and parochial schools, it did not have a monopoly on education. This decision, of course, has held until today.

As we approached the turn of the century, Johann F. Herbart's ideas became dominant. Maintaining that the aim of education was the attainment of good moral character, acquired only by analyzing the social interests of man, he presented the following formal steps of teaching and learning: 1) preparation, 2) presentation, 3) association, 4) generalization, and 5) application. These ideas filled a void in educational theory at the time, hence their dominance.

John Dewey became one of the first to raise a cry against this rigid lock-step method of schooling, seeing it as failing to account for natural growth and individual differences. He felt that schools were too antidemocratic and the curriculum too subject-centered. Popularizing *pragmatism*, he made it the philosophy of his educational reform, emphasizing the practical questions of how we can understand and control the world, rather than the metaphysical ones such as how we can know reality.

Under pragmatism, also called experimentalism, skills in problem solving and personal experience were stressed. The child was viewed as an organism interacting with his or her environment and the school as part of life itself, not merely a preparation for adult living. Freedom, according to Dewey, was a major principle of pragmatism, since the child should develop naturally and be confronted with situations in which he has a genuine interest. Dewey stressed, however, that freedom must be achieved through intelligence, apparently, already then, afraid that freedom could be misconstrued as license.

Where Are We Now?

We still feel John Dewey's influence, an influence that goes back as far as the turn of the century, when he professed that psychology, in general, and functionalism, in particular, should be applied to education. According to Dewey a child proceeds through the same thought process as a scientist. He described this process as occurring in five steps: 1) activity, 2) problem recognition, 3) data gathering, 4) formation of a hypothesis, and 5) testing. Dewey also concluded that a child must engage in genuine activities in order to learn; passive reception of lessons imposed by a teacher were not enough.

But Dewey's ideas were not the only ones to influence present-day education. Behaviorists, from John B. Watson to B.F. Skinner, added theories that the environment is of primary importance in learning and that most of our emotional responses are learned not instinctive. They brought objective evaluation and experiments into the field of learning and demonstrated (Skinner) how animals could be taught (trained) to perform complex tasks by a process of rewarding each step of progress. Their activities contributed to the application of more objective learning techniques and evaluations in education.

Gestalt or "form" psychology, imported from Germany, maintained that the essential element for learning was total recognition and understanding of the problem and environment. Important was the examination of the *pattern* received by the learner in his total environment, not individual steps or elements separately considered.

Swiss-born Jean Piaget weighed in with his efforts to develop a body of psychology which would support educational techniques. He asserted that the two fundamental characteristics of a child's learning and cognitive development were *organization* and *adaptation*. By organization, Piaget meant the systematizing of information into meaningful patterns and, like Dewy, Piaget saw human beings born as naturally active and curious, with an innate interest in communication.

In his book *Science of Education and the Psychology of the Child* Piaget urges us to recognize and follow the laws of human intelligence, present also in the child and youth. And since the functioning of the mind is the same at all ages, only qualitatively different for the child, we should help the child develop moral and intellectual reasoning power, not try to fill it with knowledge. He points out that all real learning comes through continuous assimilation of outside reality, and not from acceptance of pre-digested knowledge. Finally, Piaget makes the perceptive observation that the development of belief in *self* should not be replaced in school with belief in *authority*, and that the former can only be accomplished by genuine intellectual exchange and cooperation of children amongst themselves.

Generally, however, the beginning of our century was characterized by progressive education, based on the ideas of Rousseau, Froebel, Pestalozzi, and Dewey. And in 1919 the *Progressive Education Association* was formed, growing steadily in members and influence. By 1928, however, Dewey himself had become critical of the PEA for its lack of a social philosophy, and eventually it fragmented itself out of existence.

In the meantime, *essentialism*, led by William Bagley, gained momentum by emphasizing fundamentals. The essentialists believed that the progressives had gone too far in catering to children's interests and were ignoring basic skills needed for successful living. Not surprisingly, in 1938, at a NEA convention, the essentialists and progressives squared off in a war of words, which then lasted for years.

Other innovations began to appear, such as the Community School, which was based on John Dewey's book *Schools of Tomorrow*. These schools organized the curriculum around the lives of the students and involved the community as a primary resource for learning.

Another idea, put forward by those termed perennialists, described the ultimate goal of education as becoming a part of the thoughts and ideas that have occupied man, and been passed down, through the millenniums of his existence. They argue that the literature of Western civilization, from the days of Plato on, contains the best statement of unchanging human nature and society and therefore provides an excellent curriculum for school children at all ages. Education, they maintain, should cultivate the intellect, and only those who are able to understand the past, and benefit from the great minds that have gone before, can be of any help in facing the major issues of today. Critics argue that the idea is unscientific, bookish, past centered, and too much concerned with the subject matter for its own sake. (The books listed are called *Great Books of the Western World*. The reader is urged to form his or her own opinion after reading the brief introductory volume *The Great Conversation*, by Robert M. Hutchins.)

At the same time that teaching theory was being formed and debated, other developments deserving mention were shaping America's schooling system. Secondary education, starting after the first world war, grew steadily until it became standard for almost all children, just as the elementary school had done in the previous century. The three-year junior high school became popular and endured for its obvious benefit of separating youth, just starting adolescence, from both older and younger students. Then, in the aftermath of World War II, the federal government entered into the financing of education with the Serviceman's Readjustment Act of 1944 (G.I. Bill), which was later revived for the wars in Korea and Vietnam.

It is the controversies in education, however, in addition to the differing and sometimes competing educational philosophies, that continue to occupy and engulf us. A persistent one has been the struggle over who should control education, that is, who should decide *what* should be taught.

Since no provision was made in the Constitution, the power to create schools fell by default to the states. In spite of this, or because of this, a battle has continually raged over what powers rightfully belong to the federal government, to the states, or to local school boards. And since World War II, the trend has been for state governments to interact more and more with traditional local educational autonomy, becoming more active in certifying teachers and approving course materials and curricula. The federal government's involvement has come mainly through court-ordered desegregation plans, equal educational opportunity laws, and regulation of those programs supported by federal taxes. All three entities, however, continue to stir up the American educational soup. Even though states have usurped the right to educate, history shows many advocates for a federal system of education. In 1867, President Andrew Johnson created a Department of Education, but it was soon reduced to a Bureau, and for more than a century thereafter the *United States Office of Education* kept a low profile and concentrated on statistics. Then in the Kennedy-Johnson years it was revived, recharged with power, and placed under the Department of Health Education and Welfare. Finally, under president Carter, it became a separate cabinet-level Department of Education.

Today, federal government control accompanies each contribution of federal funds, as in the *Elementary and Secondary Education Act* of 1965. States in turn have tended to both oppose federal government control and give more and more authority to local school boards. This is understandable since local taxes usually pay the lion's share of public school costs. The problem with this development, however, is that areas of concentrated wealth enjoy a stronger tax base and hence better schools. The resulting inequality of educational opportunity, in an increasingly mobile America, has grown to be a major source of strife and contention, joining our many others.

> (The situation is exacerbated by one of our strongest fears, justified by experience, that money or control when placed in the hands of a large bureaucracy, such as the federal government, invariably produces immense waste and mismanagement. So often have these convictions been verified by actual horrors that, probably more than any single belief on earth, this one comes closest to uniting the world's humanity. In our case, we have done our best to ensure its verity by packing our institutions with mediocrity and staffing their leadership with political boon collectors. Beyond this, the personnel transience innate in these enormities has encouraged procrastination, negligence, and corruption; culprits are long gone before they can be held accountable. As a result, short-fused time bombs, such as environmental poisoning, and the Savings and Loan mass robbery, are exploding

already. Some of the more delayed but deadlier ones are yet to go off, when dangerous industrial and nuclear wastes, buried all over the country, begin in earnest to ooze their disaster upon us. In spite of these depressing facts, there is a way to use the federal government only as an equitable and centralized collector of funds, and still place control of education firmly into local hands, as we will soon discuss.)

Teacher Education

Let us now turn our attention to one of the most important elements operating from w*ithin* our educational institution. Taken as a whole, our teacher education borders on calamitous. Only the biased (those in education) and the completely uninformed would dispute this. But, although past unwillingness of professional educators to admit to the need, and undertake necessary reform, is far from admirable, the basic fault lies in the value we, as a society, have placed on education. That aspect, however, we will reserve for the section *What Should We Do?*

Without doubt our approach to teacher education has never been well thought out. It has fluctuated between requiring nearly nothing, to requiring excessive formal degrees, but rarely has it been prudent. For example, for years a shortage of teachers caused us to ignore even the small standards we had. In rural areas especially, large numbers of teachers were given certification on the basis of passing examinations, or on the strength of a year or two of college. Since at least the 1960s, however, there has been the opposite trend—to pressure for additional formal education for virtually all teachers— thereby unleashing a river of mostly useless published papers. Little of this academic flourish has benefited the student, since the emphasis has been on additional degrees not necessarily on knowledge to enhance teaching. Graduate courses in education are popular mainly because teacher salary increases are tied to acquired graduate credit hours, advanced degrees, or both.

Chapter 7 - Education   127

Even more disturbing is the swelling of the educational bureaucracy with the products of these graduate schools, again, with no resulting improvement to education.

On the other hand, and in contrast to this wrong-purposed academic effervescence, it has become almost unanimous among seasoned teachers that field experience is the most relevant and beneficial part of teacher education. They agree that one year of internship would be far better than the traditional, never-changed, one semester of practice teaching at the side of a cooperating teacher. But even this small reform goes unimplemented.

It must be mentioned, however, that the Holmes Group, a subset of the National Association of State Universities and Land-Grant Colleges, has recently undertaken the long over-due task to reform teacher education. It is investigating a *five-year* course for teacher certification in an effort to lift the standards of the profession, appearing to finally believe its own proclamation that "the future well being of the nation rests much upon our ability to recruit, educate, and retain high quality teachers."

The Educational Potpourri

To conclude our capsulation of where we are today we must also mention some of the more recent developments, influences, and studies. In the last few decades various ideas and approaches in education have been tried, but usually without concerted and coordinated effort or follow up. Generally, educators have concentrated on computer-assisted instruction, a relevant curriculum, and compensatory education for the culturally deprived. None of this, of course, has worked, and the last twenty years have seen only a worsening of our educational level, as well as the infestation into our schools of the direst of society's ills—drugs and violence.

Parallel to the above, other developments have occurred on a lessor scale, such as the growth of Montessori school programs for young children. These accelerated only in the last decade, although the educational ideas of Maria Montessori have been around since 1911. The federally-funded program Head Start has provided this type of preschool help to those unable to pay.

In addition, and for a multitude of reasons, including control of values to which children are exposed, some parents began educating their children at home. This was not accomplished without opposition. In Stephens v. Bongart, in 1937, the court found that home instruction was not equivalent to that provided in public schools, partly because of a lack of opportunity for socialization. In the Massa case of 1967, however, it was held that socialization and social development had no place in determining whether home schooling was equivalent to public education. Consequently, home schooling is now practiced nation-wide.

John Holt, influential in attempts to reform education, has been, as well, a source of help to those families undertaking the job themselves. He has urged both kinds of teachers to focus on children and their individual needs rather than upon the formal ingestion of rigid curriculum. Holt has offered practical suggestions on how to keep interest alive in schools as well as on what can be done to encourage each student to reach his or her maximum potential.

Ivan Illich, more than anyone, has shaken the pillars of educational institutions and stirred up thinking, not only by denouncing compulsory education but also by calling upon all modern nations, like the United States, to give up their public system of education. Illich feels that the right of an individual to learn is actually hampered by compulsory attendance and mass education and that it is not feasible to create schools that will actually meet the educational needs of the masses. Education is the responsibility of society and must not be delegated to schools, which are operated by governments for the benefit of the few. Yet "shaken" is probably too strong of a word when considering the immovable mass of the American educational bureaucracy and the inertia of public indifference. He has, at least, caught our attention.

Since the mid 1960s, two schools of thought have dominated the controversy over curriculum organization and content. One is the child-centered, open, free, humanistic, and socially oriented movement, grounded in the work of Dewey and A.S. Neill. To adherents of this movement curriculum content is less important than the process used and the relationship to the learner. The opposite movement calls for standardized subject matter, no-nonsense basic education, high academic standards, and discipline-oriented schools. They feel schools must concentrate on producing experts who can lead us in this ever more technological society.

In addition to the already-mentioned projects; Vista, Job Corps, Teacher Corps, and Upward Bound are federally-funded programs that were implemented to help disadvantaged students. Other innovations, found today in many elementary schools, include team teaching, non-graded schools, individualized instruction, open classrooms and programmed learning.

Furthermore, a number of curriculum additions have been introduced in an effort to address many of our other social problems. Among these are: career education; consumer education; environmental education; ethnic and multi-cultural education (designed to enhance the self-esteem of culturally different students and promote understanding by majority students); education dealing with drug and alcohol abuse; and sex education.

The Paideia Proposal was offered in 1982 and advocated giving the same quality of schooling to all. It argued for a basic and general education, with postponement of electives and specialties until college, and proposed that the basics of education provide the "skills of reading, writing, speaking, listening, observing, measuring, estimating and calculating."[4] By ensuring that all schools provided these fundamentals, colleges could then concentrate on higher skills rather than first shoring up the basics. The study program proposed was both liberal and general and gained advocates among those favoring liberal education and the teaching of thinking skills.

In addition to the various proposals and curriculum changes, studies have been conducted to analyze the results produced by today's education system. To no one's surprise they have not been encouraging. Jonathan Kozol, in his 1985 book *Illiterate America*, has pointed out that 25 million Americans cannot read the poison warnings on a can of pesticide, or read the front of a newspaper, while another 35 million read below the level necessary for success in society. His study concluded that among the member nations of the United Nations the US ranks *forty-ninth* in literacy.

A Nation At Risk, a 1983 report by the National Commission on Excellence in Education, showed that American students never reached first or second, and often were dead last, when ranked against other industrial nations on nineteen academic tests. In addition, they found that approximately 13 percent of the nation's seventeen-year-olds were functionally illiterate; among minority youth it was 40 percent. Among high school seniors, nearly 40 percent could not draw inferences from written material, and only one third could solve a mathematical problem requiring several steps. SAT tests, they reported, had declined steadily from 1960 to 1980, and some 23 million adults could not pass simple tests of reading, writing, and comprehension.

Of course, educators have fought these findings. Criticism leveled at the Commission's report charges that it offers no model for high quality education, deals little with pedagogy, and suggests "no means of implementing excellence while maintaining equality." These criticisms, however, could better be self-directed, since no concerted plan to improve education is yet to come forth from the American professional education body, only pleas for more spending. Meanwhile, of course, each proposal from outside is systematically thwarted, not for pedagogical reasons, but most often on social grounds, such as some argued disadvantage to minorities. This is exactly what is occurring today in the minimal discussions on proposed vouchers.

In other words, our professional educators, whom we still allow to direct and implement education, have been quick to criticize the reform attempts of others but have had little to offer of their own. Their responses to criticism have been to criticize the criticism, while remaining steadfast in obstructing any real reform. It seems clear, however, from all that we have said, that immediate educational reform is exactly what we need. And unless we finally cast aside their irrational objections, along with those of single-cause minority advocates, there can be little hope of instituting it. We will, instead, allow a few, adamantly and dishonorably concentrating on their own careers or causes, to push all of us closer and closer to the edge of collapse.

Where Do We Go From Here

The moment of truth has arrived; what do we do about education in America? Do we continue to try something here, try something there? Do we continue our foolish and futile efforts to please the religious right or the black minority, to use schools for everything but actual education? And do we continue to trust education to those who have totally failed in the past, and now adamantly oppose authentic reform? Or do we finally apply honest evaluations, with a goal towards coming up with the best education we possibly can?

Setting aside for the moment our dire need for education to save ourselves, isn't is time to be fair to the next generation by giving them the benefit of unfiltered education and a clear chance at improving their own future lot? After all, they will have to live with the consequences of their education longer than any of us. And we have definitely forfeited our right to tell *them* or anyone else what they should learn, or believe.

Our goal must therefore be to find a way to achieve a genuine and broad education for as many as possible, and a good first step would be to clarify what we do *not* want. History and past failures have at least brought us this far, assuming we care to read and understand their lessons. It is finally time for intellectually honest discussion, not mere talk designed to ease pressures, defend past actions or inactions, or maintain a personally favorable status quo.

What We Do Not Want

The Unbelievable Arrogance of Indoctrination

We do not want indoctrination, not by the religiously zealous, not by the politically idealistic, not by anyone. All values can and should be transferred by honest means—by good argument and by self-set example, especially in the family. The actuality that family life often takes place only evenings and week-ends, and often with only a single parent, is no argument for transferring its responsibilities to school. Schools are for learning and peer interaction and not to be used as a substitute for the family. (This is not to deny both the need and wisdom of providing nutritional and other health support at schools.)

The mere need to indoctrinate is already tacit admission of the weakness of the doctrine, or fear of its rejection. But, regardless, no one has the right, not even the U.S. government, to use the educational system to promote particular ideals, morals, political convictions, or religious beliefs. It doesn't work anyway. It should be clear by now that any moral, ideal, or conviction of any kind is only truly held when personally and voluntarily accepted. And acceptance demands far more than mere words or statements, something youth know instinctively, as evidenced by the never-ending relevance of J.D. Salinger's *The Catcher in the Rye*.

Isn't it time to recognize and admit that moral development is a process largely separated from the education system? How we see people *live*, in family and community, does far more to shape our morality. And to our great shame, most families and communities have defaulted their roles to the media, especially television.

At first television complied by broadcasting numerous, wholesome family programs. As we—our families and our education—deteriorated, television has merely attempted to keep up by providing whatever audiences desire, no matter how mindless. Contrary to what many may *want* to believe, commercial television is not the ultimate culprit. Television producers do not simply deliver junk and say: "Here, this is it, take it or leave it. This is what we think you ought to watch." To the contrary, they monitor and tests the viewing audience, eliminating what goes unwatched, while producing more and more of what is watched.

No, the real cause of deficient moral development lies within the individual adult, especially parent, who refuses to admit or confront doubts, shows little interest in learning, little interest in questioning, little interest in reading, but a great deal of interest in material goods and entertainment. These are the values that are passed along, and schools could never hope to counteract these unfortunate influences. What schools can do is present a neutral haven for enlightenment, where questions of interest can be pursued, and a supporting environment for further refining one's own ideals and morals.

Rather than indoctrination, our goal in education must be the opposite. Instead of delivering our youth into the hands of cults, sects, gangs, and various scam artists, we need to prepare and assist them in developing minds of their own. What we really want to emerge from our schools are youths and adults capable of deciding matters for themselves; not sheep who are easy prey for 900-number shams, television evangelists, absurd advertising, political commercials, lotteries, and "free gift" come-ons, all of which are thriving U.S. enterprises.

Some will no doubt argue: "but our schools are hell holes, full of crime, drugs, and learning indifference. They are carrying out indoctrination of the worst sort. If we don't do something to counteract it, all is lost." This is true and exactly what we intend to eliminate with a rational approach to education.

The Struggle For Control

Along with indoctrination, the constant struggle for control of educational decisions is deeply undermining our education. In effect, those striving for control are also endeavoring to indoctrinate, by imposing their wills upon the selection of curricula and materials. If we truly want educational reform, however, we must stop wasting time with this struggle. There is no just rationale for bestowing this power upon federal or state governments, or even upon local boards of education. In fact, it is highly presumptuousness of any person or organization to claim this right and expertise; it would even be laughable were this a laughing matter.

To quote John D. Pulliam again in his *History of Education in America*: "All through history, the progress of education has been linked to the whims of politics and public attitudes." Now is the time to finally break this linkage. But who *should* decide on curriculum and textbooks? A good question and, again, one we will soon take up.

What We Do Want

We've taken that first step and clarified what we do not want in our reformed education system. Now, let's try to agree upon what we do want. The following three statements of global desires in education are offered.

Education Available to All Who Want It

One of our long-standing principles—now taken for granted— is that public education should be available and free to everyone. To this practice we have added the requirement that it be *compulsory* until the age of sixteen. Unfortunately, the result of the latter action has been to burden the school system with baby-sitting and reform-school duties.

What we really mean, and what more closely approximates our American ideals, is that public education should be free and available to all *who want it*. Of course, the compulsory requirement was largely meant to protect children, usually from parents who might neglect educational opportunity out of economic necessity. This is still a concern today (although society has changed considerably since compulsory education became nation-wide over sixty years ago), but it can be dealt with in other ways. At issue is how to give everyone the same *access* to quality education, and this must be our focus. We can little afford to waste our energies and burden our educators with the duty to maintain order amongst the totally disinterested. Nor should school be used to keep juvenile delinquents off the street. Relief from these handicaps to teaching will constitute a major benefit to our educators, once compulsory education is eliminated and education is pursued only by those who want to learn. We will also experience additional side benefits. Without doubt, the learning atmosphere in schools will improve vastly and a sharp reduction in, if not elimination of, drugs and other crime will follow. This becomes even more self-evident when we come to agree on the purpose of education.

Education Based on Interest

As already often mentioned, it's our good fortune that learning is the natural product of interest and that the simple process of satisfying curiosity produces learning. Conversely, attempts to force learning down the throats of the unwilling has proved to be pure folly and a waste of time and effort. Most everyone who has ever been in a classroom will agree. Few of us can remember, and therefore never learned, the multitude of useless facts which we crammed into our heads in preparation for tests. For this reason alone, it must be obvious, even to the education profession, that to educate we must first create interest; we cannot simply plow ahead without it, thereby destroying its chance to eventually grow with time.

History and foreign languages are, again, perfect examples. Looking around us, we see people who have learned a foreign language or have taken up reading history; they've done it, of course, out of interest. Contrast their numbers, however, to the multimillions who for years received history and foreign languages as a steady part of their educational diet, but today exhibit little or no evidence that they were ever even exposed to either.

Clearly, anyone possessing interest learns quickly and with relish. It stands to reason, therefore, that education must respect interest above everything else, endeavoring never to destroy it and, as much as possible, to create it.

Consequently, we need educators skilled in stimulating interest but also flexible enough to synchronize with its varied chronological development in children. This is nothing new, nor is it easy to accomplish, but if we continue to ignore it we continue to doom our education, and the nation, to mediocrity.

Education That Keeps On Working

It's safe to say that no person has ever emerged "educated" from our educational system, nor will it ever happen. "Education is a lifelong process of which schooling is only a small but necessary part."[5] Only those who have managed it for themselves can truly call themselves educated, and they would not do so for they know the process never ends. What they *have* managed to acquire, however, is the ability to learn for themselves.

Learning *how* to learn means learning how to gather information, evaluate it, and organize it into meaning. It also means learning how to examine for objectivity conclusions of others and oneself. It means being alert to the dangers of attempting to answer open-ended questions (is truth good? is killing wrong?) with absolute answers, as well as being aware of the scarcity of closed areas of knowledge.

The learning process is, after all, much like the building of a house; following the foundation, a framework must be constructed, without which nothing is there to build upon, nothing to which to attach the new material. It could also be likened to the process of obtaining a map, together with a few map-reading or navigation principles. The rest is left up to the traveler; he can go anywhere he chooses.

Our goal therefore, as idealistic as it may sound, must be to produce individuals responsible for their own life-long education. Answers will not automatically be supplied whenever interest is piqued; they must be searched out and found. The purpose of education, must be to prepare us to do just this, as well as to instill confidence in our capacity to learn, evaluate, and reason.

Questions We Must Answer

It is almost time to leave theory and philosophy and suggest some practical steps. Whatever is suggested, however, must answer the three well-known basic questions of education:

Who will be educated?
What institution will control education?
Who will provide the financial support?

Nothing offered here, of course, is held to be the wisest or best; the door is wide open for better ideas, albeit with one caveat. No offered idea should incorporate what we do *not* want (indoctrination or continued strife over who controls education). These activities have been proved by history, as well as by our undisputed miserable performance in education, to be totally bankrupt. Anyone refusing to accept this will be unable to contribute much to educational reform.

It is also time to dissociate education as much as possible from our own flawed concepts and convictions and to trust much more in the powers of new generations to form their own (unflawed, we hope). The only prerequisite is that they be informed, and this is where we must place our energies. This is no risky gamble. To the contrary, it is an extremely wise move, given the existence of our own prevailing ignorant majority and our demonstrated inability to deal with contemporary problems.

But before going on to offer a new approach to education and answering the key three questions, there are additional ones we need to ask and reach agreement upon.

1. What Is The Purpose Of Public Education?

To *promote* learning, would be a good answer. The purpose should certainly not be to keep children off the streets, as mentioned above, nor should it be to fill slots in the economy; the latter is training, not education. Training merely prepares us to carry out some activity; education prepares us for living. It gives us the ability to reason and to think, which is critical to each of us, regardless of the occupation we perform.

But how does such education prepare us for anything specific? It doesn't. Primarily, it gives us confidence in our own intellect. We can ask good questions. We can evaluate offered answers for credibility and adherence to reason. We can weed out nonsense and irrelevancies and can make our own judgments. Real education shows us how to learn and gives us confidence that we can learn, can evaluate, and can reason. Once we have this "education" we can usually become trained in anything we choose (and have some aptitude for).

But if education doesn't achieve anything specific where do we get the trained people we need in modern society? No problem. Workers, even skilled technical workers, can always be trained within any political or educational system; that has already been proved. A democracy, however, is a special animal. It needs thinking people to make it work, not single-minded worker bees. It requires rational people with enough self-confidence to think along and participate. As long as we are committed to a democracy it becomes imperative that we use public education to first of all produce thinking voters; otherwise we will send it straight to an early grave.

If we cannot produce aware, functionally literate, and thinking people, it would be wise to drop both public education and democracy and concentrate on creating an enlightened aristocracy, before it is too late. At least then we will have a *few* who know how to think. It's hard to imagine a more foolish path than that of giving everyone the right to vote, while at the same time ensuring their weakness of mind through phony education. "Suffrage without schooling produces mobocracy, not democracy."[6]

If we look to Webster's dictionary we find education defined as: "to give knowledge or training to." Yet this is not what we want to accomplish, for we have already shown that we can't really *give* knowledge to anyone; they must obtain it for themselves by first having an interest. Looking at the definition of "tutor" we find exactly what we want: "direct the studies, teach and instruct". This is the best and real purpose of an educational system: to give guidance and instill confidence in learning. After that, education is a breeze. Everyone can and should do it themselves.

2. How Do People Learn?

Regardless of all else we have discovered about the human mind and the process of learning, empirically or otherwise, interest has always proved to be the key. Jean Piaget has tried to make it clear to us that the entire educational process, starting with our infancy, is a continuous effort, based on interest, to assimilate outside realities into ourselves. "Interest is nothing other, in effect, than the dynamic aspect of assimilation."[7]

We cannot get around it. Interest is not only natural, it is critical for learning. (In spite of the reality that, as Wilder Penfield and his brain probe experiments have shown, every event taken in by our conscious and concentrated mind appears to be stored somewhere in the brain.) Forced learning simply does not last, since it satisfies no basic interest or curiosity. Granted, we sometimes must resort to using it, learning the alphabet or multiplication tables, for example, but such efforts are really an attempt to fashion a tool to facilitate further learning.

It's gratifying to also note the absence of pain in the learning process when interest is present. No one need force any of us to read something we're actually interested in; it's done gladly. And once interest is present, the mechanics of learning routinely take over. Information is questioned and evaluated, and contradictions, incompleteness, and inadequacies are noted. The process of enquiring and acquiring automatically proceeds. The more we do this it seems the better we get at it, and the better educated we become.

Therefore, no matter what other methods and means are later discovered, we cannot go wrong by making interest the linchpin of our education efforts.

3. Who Should Be Responsible For Education?

The question, given today's situation, naturally anticipates one of the following responses: local board, state government, or federal government. Before answering, however, let's first break down *responsibility* further, into basic and financial. Putting aside for the moment the question of financial responsibility, we should be able to agree that *basic* responsibility for learning rests first with the individual, whether child or senior citizen, since no one else can do the learning for us. Of course, it goes without saying, that adults have the obligation to prepare children for learning, to encourage them— especially by example—and to create an atmosphere where learning is desired, admired, and rewarded.

Unfortunately, in today's *national* atmosphere, we have done little to encourage learning; our praise and rewards go elsewhere. The American dream has come to be associated with the world of entertainment and, unlike any time before, the financial rewards are great enough that merely a few years activity provides enough money to retire to the life of a millionaire.

And even though entertainers can do little to stop drug addiction, to create jobs, to achieve health care, or to save us from ubiquitous crime and violence, we adore them beyond belief, just for the diversion they provide. For this we pay each of them a fortune. (Is Boris Becker the only one questioning the sanity of a world which pays him millions just to play tennis?)

But returning to the question of basic responsibility, it is clear that, until a child is mature enough to shoulder his or her own responsibility for learning, tutoring and educational decisions must be assumed by another entity. This responsibility obviously rests first and foremost with parents, or anyone they entrust it to. There is no good reason for placing it in the hands of government or even locally-elected education boards. When we do, we are, in reality, allowing a nondescript few to make decisions for which they have already demonstrated little understanding or ability.

Of course, it could be argued that if we left education up to parents, we would accelerate our backslide, since many parents have proved to be totally inept at encouraging learning. The concern is well founded, especially given the dominance and omnipresence of entertainment.

Nevertheless, we must place some hope in the natural wish of parents not to have their children repeat their (the parents') mistakes. In effect, (we will see as we proceed) what is required from parents is the simple act of listening to and guiding the interests of their children. If they truly wish the best for them, they will finally encourage the pursuit of knowledge *in their own homes*. If they do not, *c'est la vie*. They are of no help. All will not be lost, however, as it now is, since eventually the child will take over the responsibility for his or her own education. And it will still have at its disposal books, libraries, and opportunities through documentaries to be transported both around the globe and back into history. (Entertainment videos have not yet totally displaced books at the library, but their encroachment is noteworthy.)

Clearly then, we can answer that it is the basic responsibility of all individuals to educate themselves their entire lives, and it is the responsibility and obligation of those who bring new life into the world, to give it the means to survive and learn for itself. It's common knowledge that those families who do encourage reading, stimulate interests, and engage in the joy of satisfying interest and curiosity, do the most for their children's education. They prepare them to enquire and acquire, that is, to learn, regardless of which schools or teachers they later encounter.

Not all parents, of course, will live up to this responsibility, which is all the more reason for immediate reform. At least we can have something waiting outside the home, for those children ready and willing to learn.

4. How Do We Know If Anyone Is Learning?

We could argue that the surest way is to simply examine the results produced—in our case a malfunctioning political process, a haphazard legal system, run-away criminality, unaffordable health care, botched race relations, trivia pursuit, Wheel of Fortune, and the booming value placed on baseball cards. We could then go on to argue that education will show itself to be working when this ludicrous procession begins to reverse itself—when the young (and old) turn down entertainment in favor of satisfying intellectual curiosity, when public speakers are held to real substance, rather than strings of appropriate-sounding words that mean nothing, and when only a few lost souls are more interested in the lives of entertainers than in living their own.

We could declare that education is taking hold when political TV commercials are banned, forcing candidates to speak in depth on the important issues of the day—and when we, the voters, have long enough attention spans to listen. We could assert that education has been successful when news programs begin competing for our attention by providing informative and enquiring coverage of events, unpolluted by melodramatics, trivialities, and attempts to be cute. In other words, the efficacy of education would become obvious as soon as our clouds of entertainment-induced stupor begin to lift.

Fortunately, there are ways of knowing the effectiveness of education earlier. The surest way is to ask. For example, a simple oral examination, say twice in a semester, would reveal a lot more information on whether anything is being learned than the inconsequential quizzes and tests given today. This would compare to the feed-back a tutor gets from his student; here the spoken word would be worth a thousand checked boxes.

On this subject, we see the teaching profession slowly beginning to acknowledge the inanity of multiple choice and fill-in-the-blank questions. Yet they see no other way of functioning, given the task of constantly computing grades for some forty or more students. Nevertheless, the entire exercise has nothing to do with learning, only with accounting, and today's accounting indicates educational disaster. But even if it didn't, we could never be certain whether actual learning was taking place or merely good cramming.

5. What Should Be Learned?

To reach our goal of continual self-education we must obviously provide neophytes with not only guidance and encouragement but also with certain fundamentals, starting, of course, with reading, writing, and the understanding and use of arithmetic. During and after the mastery of these, we can move on to the abundance of other subjects, but first we must lay the foundation. Such assistance begins with an introduction into the use of sources—dictionaries, encyclopedias, thesauruses—and extends to encouraging the continual exercise of the individual's thinking powers. Exercise comes about in great part through conversations at home and at school, but could take place anywhere. We must have it, however, for only exercise can produce confidence in one's reasoning powers, critical to the self-educating process.

A.S. Neill's Summerhill experiment, above all else, proved conclusively that the practice children received at Summerhill in testing their thinking and mind-working against others of all ages, produced children, youths, and later adults, who suffered no doubts or insecurities about their ability to understand, reason, and participate. In this, they stood head and shoulders above the rest of societies' members.

We can conclude then that each person needs to learn *how* to learn. To do this he or she needs some fundamentals, some guidance, some encouragement, but most of all, confidence in his or her abilities. This is exactly what our present system fails to deliver.

6. What Kind Of Teachers Should We Have?

From all that we have said so far, one quality is obviously essential—the ability to stimulate and encourage interest. Techniques can be learned, of course, but thankfully, there is a natural irrepressible source of this quality—the enthusiasm and interest of the teacher, for learning in general, and for the subject matter in particular. It has been known forever that enthusiasm for a subject is a real attention getter. Many train themselves to feign it; television is full of examples. In our teachers, however, we need the genuine kind. We need teaching professionals who actually *enjoy* learning more about everything but especially more about their own chosen subjects or field. They should love talking about their interests, as we often observe in scientists, many of whom would have themselves selected teaching, had our society treated it as a true profession.

In addition to enthusiasm, however, we require professional educators skilled in stimulating and assisting in the enquiry process. They must be adept at provoking questions and debate, and be able to demonstrate the processes of reasoning, questioning assertions, and drawing conclusions. Teachers should both encourage and be open themselves to ideas, but, although they are absolutely free to give their own opinions and conclusions, these should not be forced upon their pupils. Instead, their ideas should be discussed on a par with their students'. And, for sure, there is no place in the learning process for distorting or promoting one line of thought at the expense of others—such as disproportionately dwelling on black accomplishments or black history. (As we have already discussed, this understandable effort to repair an unjustly damaged self-image can only truly be accomplished with genuine education.)

Above all else, we need teachers who leave their students still thinking about the questions discussed in class, and with an urge to dig up more information on their own.

We have, of course, no right to expect good teachers to emerge from our present system, having made no effort to entice competent candidates into the profession, neither with adequate salaries, prestige, nor challenge. In the U.S., teaching has rarely been perceived as an important and learned profession, except at the college level. We have even, as already mentioned, qualified teachers after one or two years of college or completion of a test. Consequently, teaching, even in high school, is often performed as a part-time job, with many possessing a secondary occupation, which they go at in full force during the long summer break.

We have not demanded much from teachers and consequently have gotten little.

7. What Infrastructure Do We Need?

Perhaps our most costly mistake was to create a large education bureaucracy. Classroom teachers are nearly matched in number by the total of administrators, principals, clerical staff, and so on. (Teachers outnumber the rest by only 1.26 to 1 and for every 13.1 classroom teachers there is one administrator, principal, or assistant principal.[8]) Those in administrative positions have obviously contributed little or nothing towards encouraging interesting and innovative teaching, or improving education. And, as we all know, school superintendents and central office administrators form the apex of the bureaucratic hierarchy and also command the largest salaries. It is also clear that these career positions exist more to reward the most political in today's ineffective structure than to further the cause of education. Firmly entrenched in their prestigious positions, they appear to be most busy when stifling attempts at reform, reform which would eventually remove many of them from their lofty non-productive positions. Collectively, it is fair to say, they have been merely presiding over a system that has been rotting for years, with their principal concern being not whether students are actually getting an education, but whether it is *generally perceived* they are.

Already in some localities, Denver for instance, parents have taken over the school superintendent's function and are running things themselves.

Next come the school building administrators—the principals and assistant principals. These are the next highest paid even though they also have no direct bearing on education, with the exception of the few who also teach. If we were to keep the present system (which it is argued here we should not), we would be wise to replace them in two ways. On one hand we need someone responsible for the operation of each school building (much like a "Facilities Manager" in business) and for the basic administrative functions necessary to keep things running, such as paying salaries and bills. Second, we need an overseer of the rules and conduct of the educational process itself. This latter part of the "principal" job, with all its associated ego bolstering, could, and should, be spread among the teachers and students. They can better decide the rules of the school and enforce those rules together. Everyone attending a school should have a right to speak out and vote on any and all matters of controversy in that school. This would not only ensure the best for the entire school but, as in Summerhill, would help develop the reasoning and articulation skills, as well as the confidence, of all of its members, from the youngest to the oldest. It would also be good practice for executing the principles of self-government, and an aid towards neutralizing the over-blown esteem given to authority figures.

In any case, learning should be the concern of the individual, not superintendents and principals, whose concentration is merely on whether students are learning what they, the "education politburo", think students should learn. Busily banning and selecting books they are merely passing along their own dubious understanding, often demonstrated to be extremely limited.

Max Rafferty — A Case Study

To underscore the severity of this mentioned obstacle to education we examine one Max Rafferty, cited as an outstanding leader in public education. As California State Superintendent of Public Instruction, Mr. Rafferty had "more schools and more school children under his supervision than any other man in the country." He was also one of sixteen contributors to the book *Summerhill: For and Against* (1970).

Summerhill was an experiment in respecting the child's mind and natural desire, and ability, to learn. The entire point of the Summerhill experiment was to encourage the natural development of the child's respect for himself, his own intellect, and for others. A. S. Neill ran this school for decades and reported on it in his book *Summerhill*.

The invective that drips from Mr. Rafferty's pen in his comments on Summerhill provides an illuminating, startling, and scary insight into the kind of mind that has dominated U.S. education for decades, while presiding over its disastrous free fall. In contrast to the balanced and mature comments of each of the other contributors*, Mr. Rafferty stands astride, like a madman with a machine gun, blasting away at everything he sees or thinks he sees. He begins with a slew of colorful, if not silly, slurs ("quack", "frauds", "rot", "guff", "twaddle", all on the first page), warming up first on Rousseau before launching into a vicious personal attack on A.S. Neill.

Here is Mr. Rafferty speaking:

"Summerhill is obviously not only uncivilized but also anti-civilized."
"I would as soon enroll a child of mine in a brothel as in Summerhill."
"Summerhill may be a very pretty and permissive piece of phallic paganism, Mr. Neill, but ..."
"It's not really the headmaster's statement of principles which bothers me so much as it is his obvious hypocrisy."
"But we [in America] don't just teach the children of wealthy atheists, ..."
"[Neill does not worry about] the breakdown of our Western code of morality implicit in the spread of Neill's hedonism..."
"He's [Neill] an educational prostitute."
"... Summerhill is a dirty joke."
"... Summerhill's twin sin against the Holy Ghost of education."

Rafferty appears most enraged at Neill for not sharing his (Rafferty's) apparent religious convictions. Neill's views towards religion and sex, however, are merely honestly and rationally explained, not imposed on anyone. Rafferty thinks his should be.

On *fear*, Rafferty intones: "One wiser than Neill has said 'The fear of the Lord is the beginning of wisdom.'" He then complains that "nowhere in the Summerhill philosophy does there seem to be the merest hint that children should learn to think and act in an orderly, disciplined manner." Growing more and more incensed, if not wild-eyed, Mr. Rafferty relates to us his impression that A.S. Neill would "not only condone staged love-ins, a gang rape, or a

---

* *See* Chapter 7 Notes

Chapter 7 - Education 149

black Mass" but would preside over them himself as "Master of the Revels". He then fires his most poisonous of arrows: "Mr. Neill's blithe penchant ... betrays him into postures which only the charity of the reviewer keeps him from describing as those of a perfect ass." Rafferty finally ends with his own pathetic fantasy of Neill as a "chidharmer" suffering his punishment at the hands of God.

We need not try to juxtapose A.S. Neill's actual message against Rafferty's mouth-foaming diatribe; the reader must do that for himself. But in his criticism of Summerhill, Mr. Rafferty obviously cannot be objective; he also cannot be honest. He not only intentionally and maliciously distorts Neill, but deceitfully extracts two quotes from the Ministry of Education's essentially positive report on Summerhill, and then states "I can only bow to the Ministry's ability to recognize fraud when it sees one."

In both of Rafferty's selected quotes the next sentence would have nullified the negativity. In fact, virtually all of Rafferty's smears of permissiveness, sexual license, lack of safety, anarchy, and so on, are contradicted by this unbiased report.

"The main principle upon which the school is run is freedom. This freedom is not quite unqualified. There is [sic] a number of laws concerned with safety of life and limb made by the children but approved by the Head Master only if they are sufficiently stringent."

and

"In any community of adolescents sexual feelings must be present and they will certainly not be removed by being surrounded by taboos. They are, in fact, likely to be inflamed. At the same time, as the Head Master agrees, complete freedom to express them is not possible even if it is desirable. All that can safely be said here is that it would be difficult to find a more natural, open-faced, unself-conscious collection of boys and girls, and disasters which some might have expected to occur have not occurred in all the twenty-eight years of the school's existence."

and

> "To have created a situation in which academic education of the most intelligent kind could flourish is an achievement, but in fact it is not flourishing and a great opportunity is thus being lost. With better teaching at all stages, and above all the junior stage, it might be made to flourish, and an experiment of profound interest be given its full chance to prove itself. There remains in the mind some doubts both about principles and methods. A closer and longer acquaintance with the school would perhaps remove some of these and possibly intensify others. What cannot be doubted is that a piece of fascinating and valuable educational research is going on here which it would do all educationists good to see."

Mr. Rafferty quoted only the first sentence of the paragraph immediately above. The real act of fraud is not difficult to recognize.

No one expects total agreement with Neill's or anyone's ideas (and certainly Neill's attributing many fears to the taboo of masturbation may not be accepted as readily as his other ideas), but A.S. Neill is honest and genuine. Mr. Rafferty, on the other hand, will say anything in an apparent attempt to disguise the farce of his entire educational career. With his conferred honors and degrees, he stands before us as the strongest example of what is wrong in U.S. education. Lost souls such as Mr. Rafferty will never grasp the difference between the respect that is *earned* by integrity—that afforded by his students towards Neill—from the artificial lip service which Rafferty demands. Mr. Rafferty's idea of a successful educational system is one (God help us all) producing people who think and act as he does. But only the charity of this reviewer keeps him from describing Mr. Rafferty's position as that of a pompous ass.

It's not his fault. He himself is a product of failed education, but we cannot afford more Raffertys, not even for one more generation. And we will never have educational reform if we wait for it to arise from, or through, the entrenched monstrosity which we have thus far allowed to control education.

A Suggested New Approach

It's time for positive suggestions. New ideas and initiatives are definitely needed for there can no longer be the slightest doubt in the inefficacy of our existing educational system, or its calamitous effect on virtually every institution we have—governmental, legal, military, and so on. Our educational system doesn't serve us now; there can be no hope it will serve us adequately in the more complex future.

One of our greatest worries has always been that of maintaining our technological edge, which we and the rest of the world, until recently, accredited to our free and compulsory public-education system. Our worst fears, however, are now being realized; we are falling steadily behind the rest of the world in more and more technologies, no matter how much we attempt to refute it or how many excuses we find. It's not surprising; it's inevitable that leadership declines together with declining education. Only the lingering benefits of our past successes, together with our vast resources, prevent this reality from being more obvious.

On the other hand, reversal of the process is easily within reach, and a resurgence of learning can be just as contagious as entertainment. Using nature's gift of inquisitiveness and her ample supply of varied interests, we can expect to find pursuit of virtually every technical and scientific field that exists. We are 250 million strong; there's no danger of shortages in any field of endeavor. Totalitarian regimes readily took advantage of this natural variety of human aptitudes by spotting early, and then supporting, or coercing, their development. No one advocates doing this, but it's clear we should not fear coming up short with the trained professionals we need. The talent and potential will always be there; we need only nourish and nurture it, and we will have all the scientists, engineers, and mathematicians we can use. We will also have all the artists, statesmen, writers, educators, mechanics, electricians, and salesmen we need.

We can begin with the simple step of making education a voluntary joy, one based first on youthful interests and progressively on all other interests as they come. To accomplish this we need only provide schools where interest is aroused and satisfied and, of course, restore everywhere proper incentive for education. Both can be done by placing education under the influence of those same cherished principles we've applied to everything else, namely, those embodied in the free-market system. Only then will we bring out the best in educational ideas and teaching abilities.

There must be no doubt, however, that *total* reform of our educational system is needed, not mere tinkering. The only real cure is to repair the roots, not snip uselessly around the periphery. With this in mind, the following is a presentation of two ideas for the type of schools needed.

School Offering Number n

One good investment for an entrepreneur in education would be in the establishment of a school for young children, where they are offered a balanced day of exercise, activity, and learning. These schools, besides specializing in the basics of reading, writing, and numbers, would offer time for trying out other things of interest, as well as offer many physical activities. By striking a balance between instruction sessions, active learning, and playing periods, they would accommodate both the child's naturally short attention span and wholesome variety of interests. Such a school would permit the child to learn more in his own individual manner, and at his own pace, making a school day both fun and educational. Of course, books and quiet time would also be available for reading and individual work. Consequently, at the end of the day the child will have received his daily needs of both learning and exercise. The Japanese have already proved the wisdom of this approach. One need only follow the report *Learning from Asian Schools* in the December 1992 issue of Scientific American, to learn of the successful utilization of this common-sense knowledge. Our failure to offer such balanced full-day schools is one reason for the resort to home schooling (notwithstanding the great number of parents who do it for religious reasons). Parents consider *all* of the child's needs over the entire day. They also stimulate learning by finding books and other material, and seeking out answers together with their children. It's the best preparation one can give for later learning. But why should we *force* parents to do this? Why not provide schools that do it?

Anticipated Criticism

It is difficult to imagine much criticism to this school offering, based on all that we have learned from Dewey, Neill, Piaget, and the current success of Asian schools. Nevertheless, we must expect some to respond that this all smacks of idleness, self-indulgence, permissiveness, and so on, and that the little monsters should better be taken firmly in hand, no seat squirming allowed, and force-fed: patriotism; respect for titles and institutions; and pre-canned, often hypocritical, conclusions on morality, ethics, justice, and the like.

School Offering Number n + 1

Beyond "children-friendly" schools, which encourage and build on the natural learning instincts of the child, we need schools based on subjects of interest. For these we already have the right model —colleges and universities. These schools could be structured around the general area of learning they pursue. Each would be a depot of previously gathered knowledge and would employ teachers (and advanced learners), who can stimulate questions and assist in finding answers, and are still avid, interested learners themselves. Schools could specialize in general science, English, French, history, geography, mathematics, mechanics, biology, chemistry, astronomy, physics, or combinations thereof (a core curriculum), whatever is in demand, from the general to the specific.

Age differences need not be problematic, as those at a similar stage of learning would naturally group together. Advanced students would make ideal and enthusiastic tutors for the others, and since everyone would be challenged by and interested in the subject, it would be only natural for discussions to flow and spill over into family and social life.

No one would receive a degree from any of these schools, simply assistance in learning and a certificate of when they attended.

Anticipated Criticism 1

No degrees! How are employers going to know whom to hire?

Employers do not need the crutch, or obstacle, of "degrees"; this is a fallacy of our present system. A high school degree today simply certifies a person as capable of cramming answers to potential test questions and then reproducing them from memory by selecting from a multiple-choice list. It could also certify him as an accomplished cheater. Other than that, a high school degree certifies nothing but attendance. Employers know little of what a candidate has learned or is capable of doing until they have him in front of them and can question him.

Given the above reality, we should finally accept the fact that the burden is, and should be, on the employer to determine if a candidate's capabilities meet his requirements. The proposed *certificates of attendance*, however, will be far more valuable than a degree, since these will show both a pattern and a proof of interest, and, as we will see, each certificate will represent a significant amount of investment.

This approach also fits perfectly into the free-market system. The best firms will be those who hire the best people, which in turn will depend on how savvy they are at interviewing and assessing ability. Such a task would give new meaning and challenge to the "human resources" division of firms.

Anticipated Criticism 2

No degrees! How will colleges know whom to admit? On what basis can they judge potential to do college work, without grades and diplomas?

The answer: the absence of grades presents no obstacle at all. In their place we have the more relative college boards (Scholastic Aptitude Tests), applications, and interviews. Besides, we are now discussing an "interested" student. There should be little doubt about such a student's potential to do college work. Proof can be found in the success ratio of those entering college at a mature age. They have proved that former grades mean nothing when will and interest are present.

Furthermore, in preparing for college, our self-motivated student has already been selecting for himself the areas of knowledge and learning most necessary for pursuing his university goal. For instance, assuming the goal of an electrical engineering career, he naturally has become interested in associated subjects like math, physics, chemistry, and electricity. Already, through the process of selecting and engaging in these fields of knowledge our college candidate has prepared himself far better than his present-day peers.

Anticipated Criticism 3

This idea, if followed, could mean eventual catastrophe for higher education in America.

I bet you say that about all of us ideas! But the concern is valid, since our colleges and universities are practically the only part of U.S. education that is functioning reasonably well. The concern weakens, however, when we take cognizance of the steadily decreasing capabilities of those entering college today. SAT results have continually declined, reading ability is down, and graduates have less than ever to show for four very expensive years. The greater danger is not that we will remove the last vestige of U.S. higher education, but that we will continue the way we are, with both our educational and economic levels going down, down, down. Nothing but *drastic* rehabilitation of education will permanently reverse this, just as nothing less than a thinking majority of citizens can preserve democracy. We must do something.

There is additional rebuttal to this criticism: these new schools cannot help but *improve* our higher education. For certain, college students will be fully literate and clearly motivated. They will have already proved that, simply by selecting and following a course towards a college education. These students won't need a continuous stream of university lectures and presentations in order to learn, either. Their own interest will drive them, not simply the wish for a diploma. And the knowledge of how to learn for themselves, together with the years of practice doing it, cannot help but serve them successfully in college.

The Real Test

These are just two suggestions for change, but change we must. Everything is at stake. We are locked in the jaws of our monster of an educational system, and it is dragging us to the depths of mediocrity. We must break the death-lock and come up with an entirely new approach to education. Today's education overseers are doing nothing to stop the rapid plunge of educational levels. Instead, they are forcing the rest of the country to bow to their low standards. Textbook publishers, for example, are forced to continually rewrite their textbooks at lower readability levels because they are unable to "sell a textbook that has been written with a readability level higher than two years *below* [italics mine] the grade for which it is intended."[10]

Whatever new educational system we decide for must be one that will offer a multitude of opportunities and result in the best and most effective teachers and schools rising to the top, and the worst fading from the scene. Only the stimulation of competition can do this. Competition brings out the best in all of us. We know that. We believe that. So why be afraid to apply it to educators? Let the student be the judge of the merchandise—the product that *he* or *she* is consuming and which will shape *his* or *her* future. The real test for any school or educator should be value given proportional to amount spent, and this determination should be made by the users of the service. Such an approach cannot help but work better than anything we've ever had before, since the system will finally be based directly on *interest*. If we are still unable to produce knowledge based on a system of encouraging instead of discouraging learning, we have no hope of succeeding anyway.

Since, however, a treatise on education is not our intention we will pursue it no further, except to address the three fundamental questions of education.

1. Who Will Provide The Financial Support?

The first criticism hurled at any new idea is that no one should put forth suggestions without considering costs. Agreed. By now you have guessed that the approach suggested here is based on a voucher system.

What is a Voucher System?

The voucher system is an idea whose time has arrived. It calls for continued school financing by tax revenues, but with a major difference—parents (and students) control the spending. A voucher is a certificate issued initially to parents. Each child in the country receives an equal number for its education. All of the traditional disputes that have continually assailed us are thereby nullified; the voucher knows no racial, financial, or residential difference.

Parents present the voucher to a school of their choice and the school exchanges it for payment by the government. Although perhaps not in the existing planning, this system could continue through high school, with the student eventually taking over the right to use his or her voucher where or when he or she chooses. Unused vouchers could even be used later in adulthood.

The beauty of such a system is that everyone has an equal chance at education, if they want it. It's as equal as we can make education and still obtain excellence. It does not, as the present system does, introduce more disorder in an attempt to fuse other goals with education. Disadvantages caused by poverty and residence must be remedied *outside* of education, for if we continue to pull our education down, what possible chance do we have of eliminating poverty or slums or solving any of our problems? First we must have education.

Voucher plans were tried in the South after 1954 as a means of supporting segregated schools, but these were rightly found unconstitutional. Some states have attempted to use a voucher system for supporting parochial schools, and cases are still pending on their legal status. The system was also the subject of study by Harvard University in the 1960s. As a result of the foregoing, today's modern proposals for voucher plans guard against racial discrimination or the use of taxes to supplement tuition at expensive private schools. The voucher system is therefore no frivolous idea; it is a feasible means of obtaining equal and excellent education.

Benefits

The benefits offered are just what we seek. It is the only proposed financial scheme which establishes incentives to improve the quality of education; everything else encourages simply more of the disastrous same. It's also quite conceivable that the same existing tax structures and amounts could initially be used to finance voucher education. Financing could start, for example, with present-day collection entities transferring their revenues to a federal pot for re-distribution, in a manner similar to the dispensing of unemployment compensation. The taxing process could subsequently, in phases, be simplified and equalized by implementing centralized federal collection.

A voucher system would allow the best and most promising new ideas to be tried and permanently adopted when successful. We could never (and should never) directly adopt Germany's or Japan's system, since they are suited to the boundaries and psychology of those countries, not ours. Yet, we could benefit from specific successes they've demonstrated. For example, the already-mentioned full day of equal and alternating physical and academic activities for young children, characteristic of Japanese schools, would find equal application in this country. Schools smart enough to apply this wisdom would pick up vouchers immediately.

Finally, all parents would have a means of directly exercising their responsibility. They could choose. Schools and teachers would naturally become more effective and many alternatives in curricula and methods would be offered. Properly regulated, a voucher system could bring innovation and much-needed reform to schools and at the same time give parents much more control over the education of their children.

The Opposition

It's not surprising that most public-school educators, and organizations such as the AFT, are opposed to the voucher system. They maintain that schools would become more segregated, with middle-class parents selecting one type while the poor and minorities would be concentrated in others. Supporting reasoning for that argument is hard to imagine, unless it assumes that vouchers will be printed in colors.

It is also declared that competition between schools would foster publicity seeking by schools, and teachers would try to be popular rather than professional. This remark only makes sense if one assumes continuation of the existing state of susceptibility to absurd advertising. Such a condition, however, is exactly what we are attempting to cure by reforming education. It cannot be used to create a catch-22 argument against reform! It also reveals a cowardly and un-American opposition to competition, an understandable fear for a group which has demonstrated very little competence.

Some contend a voucher system would be unworkable and might destroy public education in the United States. We can only reply, the risk is worth it. U.S. public education has already been badly mauled and mangled; the question is whether it will survive at all. It seems our friends responsible for the damage thus far are simply pleading for more time to finish the job.

The Clear Winner

The only genuine, non-contrived, drawback to the voucher system is that it will take intelligent planning and effort. This, of course, sends a shiver down the spine of our educational bureaucracy. Their enthusiasm for reform resembles that of Russia's 70-year-old communist party.

As expected, the old standby criticism of alleged disadvantage to the urban poor, was already fired in the first salvo. It totally lacks logic. Are we to forever give up the pursuit of excellence in education every time this complaint is thrown up? Reform of education will help us all. We all need it. It is totally irresponsible to charge the voucher system with causing deeper social problems. In fact, just the opposite is true. Without a voucher system only the wealthy can *select* schools; the poor must accept whatever the local school system offers.

We all know what has been happening. Any parent worth his salt, and with the means available, uses it to get his child out of the quagmire of drugs, danger, and low-grade education and into a good school, usually private. Those without the means simply suffer our sorrowful system, and all feeble efforts to change this have failed. The situation only gets worse. It gets worse because we have used the educational system for everything but actual education. We have used it as a massive bureaucracy, offering massive numbers of civil-servant jobs. We have used it to break up segregation. We have used it as a means to eliminate ghettos. We have used it to keep juvenile delinquents occupied until the age of sixteen. We have never truly valued education for itself.

We need, of course, humanitarian social programs as stop-gap measures against poverty, until the causes can be eliminated. But the educational system is not a social program, and if we are ever to reduce the need for these programs we must not allow them to become our focal point. The focus must be kept on creating a fair environment for every one, which means a fair opportunity at education. We all need hope to keep us going, but a far more mature placement of that hope, would be in education, not the lottery.

Furthermore, the educational system cannot be used to compensate for failures of the family. Parents, regardless of their situation, cannot be relieved of their educational responsibilities, only assisted in fulfilling them. On the other hand, parents trying to do their best for their children cannot be forced, or expected, to disadvantage their children in any way because of the folly or misfortune of others.

Finally, it borders on the absurd to even listen to the weak and disingenuous arguments put forth by the traditional educational bodies. The AFT and NEA, operating principally as guilds, have proved themselves to be far are more concerned with protecting jobs than improving education, unwilling to even acknowledge the need for real reform, much less be of help in achieving it. Of course, the mere suggestion of a voucher system petrifies them, and understandably so. Such a system holds no future for many who are far below the minimum necessary level of competence. To counterbalance the voice of these unions of teachers, perhaps we should allow the students of America, say those between the ages thirteen and seventeen, to register their vote on the voucher system. After all, they have more legitimate interests at stake.

(On the positive side, as of this writing, cracks are showing in our traditional approach towards education—the Whittle Plan, offering free choice via vouchers to one thousand schools, appears headed for reality.)

2. What Institution Will Control Education?

Finally! —an end to the long frustrating battles over local versus central control, parental versus governmental management, and public-school versus private-school financial support. With the voucher system, control finally returns to the family—the parents initially, later the individual. And in exercising their responsibility, parents will have a large number of possibilities to choose from. Best of all, with interest established as the basis of learning, the disinterested and criminal will no longer be there to disrupt things, and public school will no doubt become the choice of almost all parents again.

No more arguments over government support for parochial schools either, since any school specializing in religious or political doctrine would be ineligible for the voucher system. Freedom to choose private schools would not be removed; parents could still choose alternative schools, however at their own expense. Returning educational responsibility to the parents carries the additional hoped-for consequence that many might begin to recognize, and combat, the damage that entertainment saturation is inflicting on us all. Education just might be boosted back up to its rightful position of value.

3. Who Will Be Educated?

Whoever chooses to.

Anticipated Criticism

The chief criticism of non-compulsory education would undoubtedly be the same one leveled at Summerhill: "large numbers will not go to school at all if it's voluntary." Let's look at that supposition for a moment. Since voucher responsibility is in the hands of parents until the child reaches age thirteen or so, the argument does not kick in until after this age is attained. Two problematic scenarios are possible. One, the child does not use his vouchers and does not pursue education, choosing to do something else. Two, he uses his vouchers but is disinterested in learning and squanders them by not seriously applying himself.

For the first case nothing is lost except time; the vouchers can always be used. But what are his or her other options? Work on the farm? Do nothing until old enough to get a job? But get a job at what? Let's assume the answer comes back: "a job building cars or airplanes." Our playful youth will quickly come to learn that to get such a job he will need the information and know-how that one gets, say, at a school of mechanics. But such a school would not begin at square one by giving instruction in all the prerequisites; it would also expect students to understand a certain amount of basic mathematics and physics.

Our hypothetical truant would eventually get the message that he will have to learn some other things first. But suppose he waits too long and finds himself at the age of eighteen or so having learned nothing beyond the basics? That's simply his free choice. Many others will get curious about how an engine works, ask a lot of questions, read books, go to some specialized schools where they can ask more questions and receive answers, and be building cars or airplanes a lot sooner than our playful friend, and probably a lot better.

In the second case the vouchers are simply wasted, gone forever, and that's how it should be. We certainly should not design an educational system based on the attitudes of the totally disinterested, should we? That's what we have now. Anyone who consciously wastes his or her vouchers is probably uneducable anyway.

But what about the parent who fails the child in the initial years? It is, after all, to be expected that some will. Admittedly, this is a weakness, but one we must accept, for it is simply impossible to protect against every existing human weakness or defect. Nevertheless, a safeguard does exist, since upon reaching the threshold age the child may rectify the situation by using his own vouchers.

Other critics might assert that government should step in and protect the child from the neglectful parent. Our problem, however, has been to get control of education back into the hands of parents and away from government. It is nonsense to argue the reverse out of this single fear. We cannot magically regulate behavior, only support the positive and punish the illegal. Again, however, the built-in safety feature of individual selection after a certain age, would limit the damage a parent could inflict from unnecessary delay or outright waste of vouchers.

Epilogue on Education

It's a disturbing picture we face today, but every age has probably been viewed as disturbing, and perhaps will be in the future. Even so, as we progress through the centuries, it becomes ever clearer that ignorance is our arch enemy; it kills every day. Just as clear are the benefits of education. As nothing else can, it provides us with hope for better futures, for peace, and for prosperity.

It stands to reason, therefore, that the correct struggle is always for education and against ignorance. But do we understand the difference between education and propaganda? Can we halt the curtain of ignorance, which is slowly descending upon us through our over indulgence in entertainment? The answers appear to be "no" to both questions, and on our present path there is no conceivable way we can change this. We have, however, a life preserver floating within reach, available for our rescue. But the longer we delay in reaching for education the less accessible in becomes.

Having said this, let us take stock of where we are and what we must do to effect our rescue. We need drastic school reform, complete restructure—from a system of devised curricula and tests, to one based on challenge to interest, and one that capitalizes on the ability and natural curiosity of the human brain, instead of dulling and limiting it. It is by far the best educational system we could ever devise—learning based on stimulated interest, and we will never know how many bright persons we have bored to tears or forced into crime, with our current dull, plodding system.

Reform also means halting our attempts to plan what children should learn, by selecting and censoring their textbooks, condemning them to wearisome, boring reading. We have no right to do this. That is not to say we should not provide guidance, but who among us has the right to deny information and control what is read? Why should Huckleberry Finn be declared taboo because it includes the term "nigger". This is information. This is insight into how people thought and lived. The rationale can only be that young people should not see or hear certain things because they might emulate them. Following such reasoning to its obvious conclusion, we should shield the young from all untoward things. They could then mature as pure naive creatures unable to cope or deal with reality.

Anyone still doubting that the entire system must be drastically revamped? Look again at what the present one has produced. "Twenty percent of high school graduates cannot even read their own diplomas."[11] (These are the words of the Secretary of Labor, Lynn Martin.) Each year they join the millions of others floating in the sea of our society, fresh meat for an array of unscrupulous businesses preying on their ignorance. Where else in the world (disregarding advertising for the moment) are so many enterprises based simply on the stupidity of the customer. Look at the 900 numbers offering life-important psychic advice or hot chances to speak to the opposite sex, lounging around and waiting to go "bonkers" over your call. Or a company that sells you the service of changing your social security registration when you marry. For fifteen dollars they'll accomplish for you the equivalent of a toll-free call to the Social Security Administration.

What we have presently accomplished with our present educational system is a gigantic market of naive individuals, ripe for the picking by advertising experts and con men. Let's take John Doe, average citizen. We sell him furniture and automobiles by screaming at him or by telling him "Hey, you're not John Doe, why drive his car?" Of course, he *is* John Doe if he falls for that line. For something requiring more persuasion, we use a movie idol or sports star to tell John what he should buy.

Examining the products of our institutions of higher learning we find a surprising number coming up short in communication skills, as we have already sufficiently pointed out. Even a recent series on Public Television, addressing the very problem of our dismal educational system, revealed top people in the profession miserably weak in expressing themselves correctly and coherently, more proof that we have education being carried out by the uneducated.[12]

Can we be worse off than that?

Aside from the positive movement such as the Whittle experiment, discussion on reforming our educational system sorely misses the mark. Current discussion is hung up on the question of who decides what should be learned and on the issue of national standardized testing. The *Treaty of Versailles* is used as an example of what definitely should be included in every school curriculum. We only kid ourselves. It does not matter. A simple poll would prove that. Very few will know. Only those whose interest was actually aroused (or later developed) in the first and second world wars, or the multiple rising and falling of Germany, will know.

There is also an unfortunate but growing hope that standardized testing will come to our rescue, a notion generated by the relative educational success of nations who use it, when their results are compared to ours. This is a puny effort at correcting a colossal problem.

Why not do better? Why not pull away the cataracts from our eyes and use the natural tool of curiosity? Why not carry out education as a nation the way educated families throughout history have always accomplished it—by encouraging interest, questions, and reading, from the earliest age, and then supplying the best guidance possible?

Most baffling of all, why not make a start by removing at least the most obvious handicaps to education? Right now we have bad teachers leaving good students bored, and good teachers teaching their hearts out to students who don't even listen. Obviously good teachers should be teaching to students who are interested. *Removal of compulsory education and the introduction of competitive education within a voucher system* would not only accomplish this but would break open the log jam of resistance to educational reform.

Regardless of what new cries of protest may be raised, these proposed actions clearly brush away that perpetual excuse of our professional educators, that no one has presented them with a "means of implementing excellence while maintaining equality."[13]

* * *

The following is offered as a splendid example of the fun and challenge of logical reasoning. It is taken from the German publication *88 Neue Logeleien von Zweistein* and reprinted here in English with permission from the publishers: F.A. Herbig Verlagsbuchhandlung, Thomas-Wimmer-Ring 11, 8000 München 22, Germany (ISBN 3-485-00446-4, pp. 11-12). It should provide an enjoyable challenge for the entire family!

* * *

Once I was at a party together with seven married couples who all knew each other very well. Consequently, I, being the only stranger, got to know only their first names and a few other things.
The men had the first names Bob, Gary, Oscar, Richard, York, Victor, and Willy. The names of the women were: Betty, Gwendolyn, Olivia, Ruth, Yvonne, Viola, and Wanda. I should also mention that each woman wore a different-color dress. The colors of the dresses were: blue, green, orange, red, yellow, violet and white. Strangely enough, none of the couples had matching first initials and also the first letter of the dress color of each woman was different from either her husband's or her first initial.

In order to find out who was married to whom I asked only the wives questions. Here are their answers:

B: 1. "Gwendolyn is wearing the violet dress." 2. "I am married to Richard." 3. "Wanda's husband always lies."
G: 1. "If you ask Oscar whether Gary is married to Betty he will say 'yes'." 2. "Willy always lies." 3. "York's wife is wearing blue."
O: 1. "If you ask Richard whether Ruth is wearing the yellow dress, he will say 'no'." 2. "In response to the question whether Willy's wife is wearing the violet dress, Gary will say 'yes'." 3. "To the question whether Viola is wearing the yellow dress, Betty would answer 'yes'."
R: 1. "If you ask Victor whether Yvonne is wearing the violet dress he will answer 'yes'." 2. "Victor's wife is wearing orange."
Y: 1. "Gary's wife is wearing orange." 2. "When asked whether Gwendolyn is Victor's wife, my husband will answer 'no'."
V: 1. "Oscar is not Wanda's husband." 2. "If you ask Betty's husband whether Ruth is York's wife he will say 'yes'." 3. "If you ask York whether Richard's wife is wearing yellow, he will answer 'yes'."
W: 1. "Oscar always tells the truth." 2. "Bob's wife is not wearing white." 3. "If you ask Betty whether she is Willy's wife, she will answer 'no'."

Each of the fourteen guests either always spoke the truth or always lied and from each couple only one spouse is a liar. Who is married to whom and which color dress did each woman wear?

* * *

(Answer on next page.)

Answer to "Logeleien":

Bob is married to Olivia who is wearing a White dress.
Gary is married to Betty who is wearing a Yellow dress.
Oscar is married to Viola who is wearing a Red dress.
Richard is married to Wanda who is wearing a Blue dress.
York is married to Ruth who is wearing a Green dress.
Victor is married to Gwendolyn who is wearing an Orange dress.
Willy is married to Yvonne who is wearing a Violet dress.

The liars are Bob, Oscar, York, Betty, Wanda, Gwendolyn and Yvonne.

Hint: *Examine the second statement of Yvonne: "When asked whether Gwendolyn is Victor's wife, my husband will answer 'no'." Either Yvonne or her husband is a liar. If Yvonne is telling the truth, then her husband would be lying in stating that Gwendolyn is not Victor's wife. If Yvonne is lying, then her husband would not answer "no" but "yes" and would be telling the truth. Either way, Gwendolyn is married to Victor and, of course, is not wearing either a green or violet dress.*

Bibliography

Baird, Robert M. and Rosenbaum, Stuart E. *The Ethics of Abortion.* Buffalo, New York: Prometheus Books, 1989.
Dacey, Norman F. *How To Avoid Probate!* New York: Macmillan Publishing Co., 1980.
Consumer Reports. *The Crisis in Health Insurance. Part 1*: August 1990. *Part 2*: September 1990.
Copperman, Paul. *The Literacy Hoax — The Decline of Reading, Writing, and Learning in the Public Schools and What We Can Do About It.* New York: William Morrow and Company, Inc., 1978
Durant, Will. *Our Oriental Heritage.* New York: Simon and Schuster, 1954.
Esperti, Robert A. and Peterson, Renno L. *Loving Trust.* New York: Penquin Books, 1988.
Faux, Marian. *Roe v. Wade.* New York: Macmillan Publishing Co., 1988.
Hentoff, Nat. *Does Anybody Give A Damn? — Nat Hentoff on Education.* New York: Alfred A. Knopf, 1977
Hertsgaard, Mark. *On Bended Knee.* New York: Farrar Straus Giroux, 1988.
Hirsch, E.D. Jr. *Cultural Literacy — What Every American Needs To Know.* Boston: Houghton Mifflin Company, 1987
Holt, John. *How Children Learn.* New York: Dell Publishing Co., Inc, 1967, 1983
Hutchins, Robert Maynard. *The Great Conversation — Great Books of The Western World.* Chicago: Encyclopaedia Britannica, Inc. 1952, 1982
Illich, Ivan. *Deschooling Society.* New York: Harper and Row, 1970, 1971, 1983.
Johnson, Haynes. *Sleepwalking Through History — America in the Reagan Years.* New York: W.W. Norton and Company, 1991.

Jones, Beau Fly. *Strategic Teaching and Learning: Cognitive Instruction in the Content Areas.* Elmhurst, IL: North Central Regional Educational Laboratory.

Journal of the American Medical Association. May 15, 1991 — Volume 265, No. 19.

Kohl, Herbert. *On Teaching* New York: Schocken Books, 1976

McLuhan, Marshall and Fiore, Quentin. *The Medium is the Massage.* New York: Random House, 1967.

Neill, A.S. *Summerhill.* New York: Penquin Books, 1962.

Postman, Neil. *Amusing Ourselves To Death.* New York: Penquin Books, 1986.

Postman, Neil. *Conscientious Objections: stirring up trouble about language, technology, and education.* New York: Alfred A. Knopf, Inc., 1988.

Postman, Neil and Weingartner, Charles. *Teaching as a Subversive Activity.* New York: Delacorte Press, 1969.

Pulliam, John D. *History of Education in America.* Columbus, Ohio. 1987

Spring, Joel. *The American School 1642-1990.* New York: Longman, 1990

Summerhill: For and Against — Outstanding writers in education, sociology, and psychology evaluate the concepts of A.S. Neill. New York: Hart Publishing Company, Inc., 1970

Tribe, Laurence H. *Abortion: The Clash of Absolutes.* New York: W.W. Norton & Company, Inc., 1990.

Wallace, Nancy. *Better Than School.* Burdett, New York: Larson Publications, Inc., 1983.

Weinberg, Meyer. *A Chance To Learn — A history of race and Education in the United States.* New York: Cambridge University Press, 1977

White, Merry. *The Japanese Educational Challenge — A Committment to Children.* New York: Collier MacMillan Publishers, 1987

Zimring, Franklin E. & Hawkins, Gordon. *The Citizen's Guide to Gun Control.* New York: Macmillan Publishing Co., 1987.

* * *

Chapter Notes

Chapter 1:
The State Of The Union's People

1. "You've heard about killer bees ...": Washington D.C. radio, 30 July 1992.
2. "This is Tom Brokaw ...": NBC Nightly News, 29 July 1992.
3. Not to be left out, Dan Quayle ...: As reported on the McNeil/Lehrer Newshour, both the president and vice president discussed the important matter of a Murphy Brown TV episode featuring a woman giving birth out of wedlock.
4. "Soft money", declared for the purpose ...: Described in Charles R. Babcock's article in the Washington Post, *Both Parties Raise Millions in `Soft Money'*, on 26 July 1992.
5. Large corporations, such as U.S. Tobacco Company, ...: Listed as top donors to three Democratic Party committees from 1988 through June 1992 are National Educa-

tional Association, as the number two donor with $582,000, and the American Federation of Teachers, as the number ten donor with $296,000. Top donor to three national Republican Party committees was Archer Daniels Midland with $1,157,000.: Ibid.
6. Benjamin Ginsberg, chief counsel for ...: Ibid.
7. "only half of California adults ...": These survey results reported in Haynes Johnson's *Sleepwalking Through History: America in the Reagan Years* (New York: W.W. Norton and Company, 1991), p. 452.
8. out of 24,000 international students ...: Ibid., pp. 452-453.
9. That goes for Carl Sagan ...: as demonstrated while narrating a program on astronomy.
10. "There's two reasons ...": Sen. Patricia Schroeder (D), Public Television on or about 20 May 1992.
11. "There's two pieces ...": Sen. George Mitchell, (D), Public Television on or about 20 May 1992.
12. "There is aspects ...": Les Aspin, Public Television on or about 25 Sept. 1991.
13. "There's three ...": Leon Panetta, Rep. (D) California, Public Television on or about 29 Jan. 1992.
14. "There's two ways ...": Sen. Jack Kemp, Public Television debate on 11 Sept. 1992.
15. "There's lots of ...": George Bush, Monitor Radio on 7 Aug. 1992.
16. "the rarest kind of ability ...": Johnson, op. cit., p. 322.
17. Reagan's only contribution ...: paraphrased from a quote by Lee Hamilton, Ibid., p. 303.
18. admitted receiving $420,000 ...: Ibid., p. 180.
19. 131 separate investigations pending ...: Ibid., p. 178.
20. "some kind of a correction" ...: Ibid., p. 385.
21. "We did not—repeat—did not trade ...": Ibid., p. 297.
22. He, of all people, he who knew dangerously little of any thing ...: Paul Slansky, writer for the New Republic, has published numerous gaffes by Ronald Reagan which reveal the extent of Reagan's general knowledge. These were published in various editions of the magazine. He has also written a book on Ronald Reagan. Some of Paul Slansky's accumulation of Reagan Quotes:

(a) Asked by reporters in October 1983 what he would do about the situation in Cyprus he said, "Oh, I wish the secretary of state were here."
(b) When Marcos stole the election from Aquino Reagan's interpretation was that it was "evidence of a strong two-party system" in the Philippines. (c) When asked in June 1985 how his tax plan would simplify the tax laws: "Wow! You know, I may turn my head here to Don Regan again.... For me to try and off the top of my head bring up some of the other benefits, now, wait a minute."
(d) In October 1982 he spoke of U.S, delegations, "two of which are in Geneva, and one, I believe, still in Switzerland."
(e) In August 1984, after a simple question about arms control, he stood speechless for several seconds, nodding and grunting and shrugging until his wife cued him with a whispered "Doing everything we can." Reagan then declared "We're doing everything we can."

23. "It's my job ...": Mark Hertsgaard, *On Bended Knee* (New York: Farrar Straus Giroux, 1988), p. 62.
24. Studies show 12 percent ...: National Public radio, May 1992.
25. A study is reported as showing 34 percent ...: National Public Radio, 20 or 21 May 1992.
26. "There is absolutely no ...": Marshall McLuhan and Quentin Fiore, *The Medium is the Massage* (New York: Random House, 1967), p.25.

Chapter 2:
Abortion

1. carried out illegally or by a sympathetic physician ...: Laurence H. Tribe, Abortion: The Clash of Absolutes (New York: W.W. Norton, 1990), pp. 34-35.
2. "the pregnant woman can not be isolated ...": Marian Faux, *Roe v. Wade* (New York: Macmillan Publishing Company, 1988), p. 52.

Chapter 3:
Race Relations

1. as jurors they have been known ...: Gabriel Escobar, "Crash Ends D.C. Convict's Escape Try", *The Washington Post,* 28 Aug. 1991.
2. A recent article in the Washington Post ...: John Rankine, *A Call for "Higher Order" Thinking,* 4 Aug. 1991, Book World, p. r19.
3. "C: How would you compare ...": Paul Copperman, *The Literacy Hoax* (New York: William Morrow and Company, Inc., 1978), p.261.

Chapter 4:
Crime and Violence

1. Already in 1970 it was four times as dangerous...: Zimring and Hawkins, *The Citizen's Guide to gun Control* (New York: Macmillan Publishing Co.,1987), p. 3-4.
2. In 1990, out of 20,045 murders ...: *The 1992 Information Please Almanac*, 45 th ed., Houghton Mifflin Co., Boston and New York, p. 954.
3. 24,703 murdered in 1991 ...: *The World Almanac & Book of Facts 1993* (New York: Pharos Books) [Source: Uniform Crime Reports, FBI], p.950.
4. Murder had already claimed twice as many ...: NOVA Video Tape, *Anatomy of Murder,* WGBH Educational Foundation, 1981.
5. "no relationship between the availability of guns and murder ...": Dr. Paul H. Blackman, Research Coordinator for the NRA, Ibid.
6. The Life and Death of the Brady and Anticrime Bills:

Chapter Notes   177

The following is taken from reports in the Congressional Quarterly following the voting throughout 1991. HR 7, known as the Brady bill, passed the House by 239-186 vote on 8 May 1991 and called for a 7-day cooling off period during which a gun purchaser would have to wait before taking possession of a handgun. During this period a background check could be made. In addition, the Brady bill prohibited the sale and import of assault-style weapons. It was sent to the Senate where it eventually became part of Crime Bill S1241, and was amended to a 5-working-days wait which was to be phased out after 2 1/2 years and be replaced with an instant-check system. The ban on assault weapons was to expire in 3 years. The Senate Crime Bill (S1241), an all-encompassing anti-crime bill loaded with ninety amendments accepted during floor action, was passed on 11 July 1991 in a 71-26 Senate vote. It required three attempts before cloture was accomplished by a 10 July 1991 vote. On that day the NRA urged Senators (as usual) to reject cloture saying that the Brady bill and assault weapon ban was "nothing less than an unmitigated attack on the right of law-abiding gun owners." [CQ 7/13/91, p. 1899] S1241 was not remarkably different from previously passed crime bills. It would authorize more money for prisons and law enforcement, expand the death penalty to dozens of crimes, among them the murder of a Member of Congress, the Cabinet or Supreme Court or a family member of a federal official [Author's note: A perfect example of congress legislating for itself, not the people.] and stiffen penalties for drug and firearm crimes. This crime bill, however, included a waiting period for handgun purchase and a ban on certain assault-style weapons. The House passed its version of an omnibus anti-crime bill, HR3371, on 22 Oct. 1991. When the two bills went into conference (24 Nov.), house and senate conferees proceeded to differ on virtually every issue, split along party lines. On 27 Nov., facing a Senate filibuster and presidential veto,

7.   the House eked out a 205-203 passage of the bill. That same day the Senate failed to stop a Republican-led filibuster against the bill, 49-38 , so the bill was dead.
"I discovered what an ideological straightjacket ...": Les AuCoin, *Confessions of a Former NRA Supporter,* Washington Post, 18 Mar. 1991, p. A11.
8.   "My Daddy Shot My Mommy", all three quottations taken from the Washington Post, on 27 October 1992.
9.   "... gunman wearing a ski mask robbed a gas station ...", all quotations are taken from the crimes reported during the period 13 th through 20 th of October, 1992 in Prince George's County, Maryland. Washington Post, 29 October 1992, pp. Md. 9-10.
10.   over 45 percent of our Senate and House ...: 61 of 100 Senators, 182 of 435 U.S. Congressional Representatives as taken from the *Congressional Staff Directory for 1991,* Staff Directories Ltd., Mt. Vernon, VA.
11.   the U.S. supports two-thirds of all the lawyers ...: Norman F. Dacey, *How To Avoid Probate* (New York: McMillan Publishing Co., 1980), p. 9.
12.   Today's Attorney General sees the solution in ...: Attorney General William P. Barr speaking on the McNeil/Lehrer Newshour on or about 24 Feb. 1992.
13.   "Murder is the ultimate human tragedy ...": Former Attorney General Ramsey Clark on NOVA Video Tape, *Anatomy of Murder,* op. cit.

Chapter 5:

Health Care

1.   U.S. trails 23 other nations ...: "The Crisis in Health Insurance", *Consumers Report,* Aug. 1990, p. 534.
2.   from 37 percent in 1984 to 24 percent ...: Ibid. p. 535.
3.   By 1990 only 22 of 74 Blue Cross ...: Ibid. p. 541.
4.   in 1988 the association spent 5.3 million ...: "The Crisis in Health Insurance — Part 2", *Consumers Report,* Sept. 1990, p. 609.
5.   health care is a privilege not ...: Ibid. p. 615.

6. guess who was the number two PAC contributor ...: Last year's top two PAC contributors: the Teamsters Union with $1.3 million and the Association of Trial Lawyers with almost $938,000 (out of a total of $73 million given to PACs over 15 months) as reported on National Public Radio on or about 7 June 1992.
7. 525 percent increase in 10 years ...: The Universal World Almanac 1990 (Kansas City, New York: Andrews and McMeel), p. 217.
8. cost an estimated annual $429 million ...: Ibid. p. 216.
9. 31 percent by insurance companies ...: Ibid.
10. [Canadian] physician incomes are still ...: op. cit., Sept. 1990, p. 615.
11. Canada spends less on administration ...: Ibid., p. 614.
12. For example, a resident of Ontario ...: Ibid., pp. 616-617.

Chapter 6:
Governing Ourselves

1. "My frustration is...": Bob Hogan speaking about his political campaigning in Youngstown, Ohio, as reported by Johnson, op. cit., p. 429.
2. "You have to make the case ...": Ibid., p. 394.
3. "The world may never know ...": John Mintz and David Von Drehle, "Why Perot Walked Away", The Washington Post, 19 July 1992, p. A18.
4. "Some 150 ads per day ...": National Public Television on or about 18 Feb. 1992.
5. *Vote Smart* information broadcast by Judy Woodruff over Public Television during the McNeil/Lehrer Newshour, in July 1992.

Chapter 7:
Education of Another Kind

1. "less than five percent of its seventeen-year-olds can ...": *The 1992 Information Please Almanac,* 45 th ed. (Boston: Houghton Mifflin Company), p. 42.
2. "21 million adults cannot read even ...": Ibid.
3. "forty percent cannot read at ...": Ibid.
4. "skills of reading, writing, speaking ...": Mortimer J. Adler, *The Paideia Proposal* (New York: Macmillan Publishing Company, 1982), p.26.
5. "Education is a life-long process ...": Ibid. p. 10.
6. "Suffrage without schooling produces ...": Ibid, p. 3.
7. "Interest is nothing other, ...": Jean Piaget, Science of Education and the Psychology of the Child (New York: Otion Press, 1970), p.158.
8. Classroom teachers are nearly matched ...: The figures given are taken from the latest figures printed in the *Statistical Abstract of the United States, 1991 — The National Data Book,* published by the U.S. Department of Commerce, 11 th ed.
9. The following are excerpts from the comments of each of the other contributors to the book *Summerhill: For and Against:*

The educational critics have, of course, had their fun with Summerhill. Their terror of the idea is probably the most accurate measure of its validity. The eunuchs have always been afraid of life. Many critics from the official academic world read books with the idea of finding what is wrong with them. My more pragmatic colleagues from the world of commerce read books to find what is right with them.

— Reverend John M. Culkin, priest, Ph.D. Education, Director of the Center for Understanding Media.

It is more than doubtful — it is inconceivable — that Summerhill could exist without Neill. Whether one agrees or disagrees with him (and only the most computerized misanthrope could totally disagree with him) the fact is that he is a man of saintly strength and force.
— Fred M. Hechinger, Education Editor of New York Times, and author.

The important thing about Summerhill is that the ideas that made and maker it work helped a great many people to understand several essential truths.... (1) the necessity of love, (2) that the only healthy discipline is the discipline of self, self-discipline, (3) that freedom is a great responsibility; and that (4) among other things, a good teacher teaches his children these specific truths, as well as teaching them how to teach themselves.
— Ashley Montagu, Ph.D., foremost anthropologist and author.

Summerhill is an infuriating book. It infuriated me when I first read it, and it infuriates me today. ... In spite of this I do have considerable respect ... for Mr. Neill... I respect his sincerity—there's nothing phony about him ... I respect the consistency of his approach ... I respect his obvious love for children ... I believe that Mr. Neill, whatever his basic theories, is a dedicated human being and a born educator.
— Louise Bates Ames, author, former director of Research for the Gessell Institute of Child Developmental Yale University, and author.

Because Neill's reaction is immediate, personal, and authentic, not impersonal, bureaucratic, and assumed, it is instructive. Now and then, as when a child swipes one of his garden tools just when he needs to use it, he may get angry. His anger conveys to children what really is wrong about stealing—that it hurts the person you steal from.
— John Holt, teacher, author, lecturer.

"... and so grossly have Neill and his work been misunderstood, that I can only strongly advise re-reading him as I did with today's educational problems in mind I urge this especially for everyone concerned with the well being of children, and for those specifically interested in what we do wrong in our methods of education.
    — Bruno Bettelheim, Ph.D., Professor of Education, Professor of Psychology and Psychiatry and author.

No one in his right mind would doubt that Neill is one of the all-too-few genuine friends of childhood.
    — Eda J. LeShan, author

In *Summerhill's* importance should be measured less by the tributes of educators and by the fact it has been widely adopted as a college text, than by its popularity among America's young.
    — Michael Rossman, educational activist

Neill has made radical changes in two sectors: structure and teaching. He has successfully combatted several educational archaisms, and he has replaced them with his own distinctive personality. We learn a lot from him what is bad in education. We do not learn enough from him as to what we can do to better the situation.
    — Ernst Papanek, Ph.D., Professor of Education, and author

A.S. Neill's pioneer experiment at Summerhill has demonstrated what freedom (not license) can do to transform the petty tyranny of most elementary and high school classrooms.
    — Goodwin Watson, Professor Emeritus of Social Psychology and Education at Columbia University, and author.

The likelihood is that A.S. Neill's hope, too, will be badly realized.
— Paul Goodman, teacher, lecturer, and author.

(*Note*: Mr. Goodman chose to concentrate on his own notions concerning education. There is relatively little said about Summerhill.)

For me Summerhill is a poetic vision. As such, I am all for it. Who can quarrel with the idea? Who would want to?
— Nathan W. Ackerman, Professor and author.

Neill's basic precept is no other than love of life ... *Summerhill* is an expression of biophilia ... One can understand biophilia fully only by comparing its opposite: necrophilia ... the necrophilous person is fascinated by all that is not alive. He likes to talk about sickness, death, burials, money, gadgets, and punishment ... Neill has the courage to show what results if one takes "living" seriously and stops gilding his alleged aims. Any critique of Neill's work must fall within this purview. Otherwise, such criticism is mere hitting out against an educational system whose essence one does not comprehend.
— Erich Fromm, Ph.D., Psychologist and writer.

10. "sell a textbook that has been written ...": Paul Copperman, *The Literacy Hoax* (New York: William Morrow and Company, Inc., 1978), p.81.

11. "Twenty percent of high-school graduates ...": Secretary Lynn Martin speaking on the McNeil/Lehrer Newshour in Jan. or Feb. 1992.

12. Even a recent series on Public Television ...: "Learning in America", on Maryland Public Television on or about 6 Jan. 1992.

13. "means of implementing excellence ...": John D. Pulliam, *History of Education in America* (Columbus, Ohio: Merrill Publishing Company, 1987), p.228.

*I have striven not to laugh at human actions,
not to weep at them,
nor to hate them,
but to understand them.*
 —Baruch Spinoza

Index

A

ABA. *See* American Bar Association
ABC (American Broadcasting Company), 27
abortion, 33-41
addiction, drug/alcohol, 82, 85
Affirmative Action, 44-46, 49-52, 55
AFL-CIO, 88, 109
AFT. *See* American Federation of Teachers
Agricultural Department, 24
Alexander the Great, 111, 115
AMA. *See* American Medical Association
AMA president, 81
American Bar Association, 66, 88
American Federation of Teachers, 19, 160, 162
American Medical Association, 77-78, 80, 86-88, 94
antiabortionists, 35-37, 40
Aquinas, Thomas, 117
Archer Daniels Midland, 17
Aristotle, 114-117
Arizona, 109
Arsenio Hall show, 14
Aspin, Les, 20
Association of Trial Lawyers, 83
Attorney General, 23, 69
Atwater, Lee, 98
AuCoin, Les, 61
Austria, 74

B

Bacon, Francis, 118
Bagley, William, 123
Bakker, Jimmy, 29
Basedow, Johann, 120
Becker, Boris, 141
behaviorists, 122
Belfast, 58
Belgium, 74
Blue Cross and Blue Shield, 79
Boesky, Ivan, 25
Brady bill, 60
Brokaw, Tom, 13
Brown, Jerry, 104

Bruno, Giordano, 118
Bureau of Land Management, 25
Bush, George, 14, 17, 20, 98, 110

C

California, 18, 88, 147
Canada, 74
Canadian health care system, 80, 83, 90, 92
capital punishment, 67-69
Carter, Jimmy, 125
CBS (Columbia Broadcasting System), 13
Chicago, 25, 49
Chinese, 39
Civil Rights Act, 44, 45
Clark, Ramsey, 72
Constitution - Amendments, 62
Consumer Product Safety Commission, 24
contingency fee, 65, 67, 82
Copernicus, Nicholas, 118
Copperman, Paul, 53
crime, 57-72
criminal rehabilitation, 69

D

Dacey, Norman F., 66
Deaver, Michael, 24
Denver, 146
Department of Education, 125
Department of Health Education and Welfare, 125
Descartes, René, 55, 118
Desert Storm, 110
Detroit, 58
Dewey, John, 121-123, 129, 153
drug addiction. *See* addiction, drug/alcohol
drug and alcohol abuse, 129
Duke, David, 52
Durant, Will and Ariel, 113
Dutch health care system, 92

E

Economic Development Administration, 25
education, 55, 111-69
education, black, 47-48
education, control, 162-63
education, family, 55
education, financing, 157-58
education, infrastructure, 146-47

education, reform, 151-68
education, responsibility, 140-42
Elementary and Secondary Education Act of 1965, 125
entertainment, 98, 101, 112-13, 141
Environmental Protection Agency, 23, 24
EPA. *See* Environmental Protection Agency
Esperti, Robert A., 66
essentialists, 123
experimentalism, 121

F

Face the Nation, 98
Federal Aviation Administration, 24
Federal Emergency Management Agency, 24
Federal Home Loan Bank Board, 24
Federal Reserve Board, 25
Fiore, Quentin, 32
fire-arm violence, 82
firearm injuries, 85
France, 74
Franklin, Ben, 119
Froebel, Friedrich, 119, 123

G

Galileo Galilei, 118
German health care system, 92
Germany, 51, 74, 92, 167
Gestalt, 122
Ginsberg, Benjamin, 17
Gralnick, Jeff, 27
Great Britain, 90
Grenada, 26

H

handguns, 58-61, 63-65, 72
Harvard University, 158
Head Start, 128
Health and Human Services Department, 24
health care, 73-94
Health Care Cost Management Firms, 77, 80
health insurance, 19, 73, 75-76, 78, 91, 93
Health Insurance Association of America, 88
Herbart, Johann, 120, 121
Hertsgaard, Mark, 27
high school, first, 120
Holmes Group, 127
Holt, John, 128
home schooling, 128, 153

Housing and Urban Development, 24
Huckleberry Finn, 165
HUD. *See* Housing and Urban Development
Hutchins, Robert M., 124

I

Illich, Ivan, 128
illiteracy, 46, 130
infant mortality, 74
insurance companies, 76-78, 83, 86
Iran-Contra, 25
Israel, 74

J

Jackson, Jesse, 44
Japan, 47, 51, 64, 152, 159
Jenkins, James, 24
Job Corps, 129
Johns Hopkins, 120
Johnson, Haynes, 105
Johnson, Lyndon, 44
judicial system, 63-67

K

Kalamazoo Case, 120
Kemp, Jack, 20
Kenya, 107
Kepler, Johannes, 118
Kimball, Richard, 109
Kozol, Jonathan, 130
Kurds, 110

L

Lasch, Christopher, 114
lawyers, 64, 66-67, 82, 83
Legal Services Corporation, 24
Lehrer, Jim, 99
Leonardo da Vinci, 118
Levine, Dennis, 25
Liman, Arthur, 26

M

mal-practice insurance, 87
Martin, Lynn, 166
Massa case of 1967, 128

Massachusetts, 118, 120
McLuhan, Marshall, 32
McNeil/Lehrer Newshour, 99
Medicaid, 79, 86
Medicare, 79, 90-91
Meese, Ed III, 23-24
Meet the Press, 98
Merrill Lynch, 17
Michigan, 120
midwives, 35
Milken, Michael, 25
Ministry of Education, 149
minority students, 53
Mitchell, George, 20
Montessori school, 128
Morrill Act, 120
murder, 68, 72

N

National Association of State Universities and Land Grant Colleges, 127
National Commission on Excellence in Education, 130
National Education Association, 19, 120, 123, 162
National Fraternal Order of Police, 60
National Public Radio, 28
National Rifle Association, 58-61, 72
NEA. *See* National Education Association
Neill, A.S., 129, 144, 147-50, 153
Netherlands, The, 74, 84
New Jersey, 62
New York, 62, 99
Newton, Sir Isaac, 118
Nixon, Richard, 26
Nofziger, Lyn, 24
North, Oliver, 25-26
NRA. *See* National Rifle Association
NRC. *See* Nuclear Regulatory Commission
Nuclear Regulatory Commission, 23, 24

O

Occupational Safety and Health Administration, 25
Old Deluder Satan Act, 118
Oregon, 108

P

PAC. *See* Political Action Commitee
Paideia Proposal, 129
Paine, Thomas, 11
Panetta, Leon, 20
Penfield, Wilder, 140

PEA. *See* Progressive Education Association
Pepper Commission, 80
Perennialists, 123
Perot, Ross, 100
Pestalozzi, Johann H., 120, 123
Peterson, Renno L., 66
Phillip Morris, 17
Piaget, Jean, 122, 139, 153
Plato, 114, 123
police brutality, 71
Political Action Committee, 83
political commercials, 102-03, 108, 133
Postal Service, 24
Postman, Neil, 30
PR. *See* Public Relations
pragmatism, 121
pre-natal, 84
press, 64, 106,110
preventive medicine, 84, 90, 91
pro-choice, 37
probate, 82
Progressive Education Association, 123
progressives, 123
public education, 121
public education, compulsory, 151
public education, purpose, 138
Public Relations, 77, 80, 100
Public Television, 101, 104, 108, 166
Pulliam, John D., 134

Q

Quayle, Dan, 14

R

race relations, 43-56
racism, 49, 53
Rafferty, Max, 147-50
Rankine, John, 53
Raspberry, William, 54
Rather, Dan, 13
Reagan, Ronald, 22-23, 25-27, 61
rehabilitation of criminals, 69, 70
Republican National Committee, 17
Roberts, Oral, 29
Roberts, Thomas M., 23
Roe v. Wade, 36-37
Rousseau, Jean Jacques, 123, 148
rubella, 35
Rudman, Warren, 30

S

S&L. *See* Savings and Loan Industry
Sagan, Carl, 20
Salinger, J.D., 132
San Francisco, 35
Sanders, James, 24
SAT. See Scholastic Aptitude Test
Savage, Gus, 49
Savings and Loan Industry, 26
SBA. *See* Small Business Administration
Scholastic Aptitude Tests, 130, 155-56
school superintendents, 147
Schroeder, Pat, 20
Scientific American, 153
secular humanism, 118
Security and Exchange Commission, 25
Serviceman's Readjustment Act of 1944 (G.I. Bill), 124
Shiites, 110
Skinner, B.F., 122
Small and Disadvantaged Business Program, 24
Small Business Administration 24
Social Security Administration, 25, 166
socialized medicine, 84, 90, 93
soft money, 16
South Africa, 93
Spinoza, Baruch, 184
Stephens v. Bongart in 1937, 128
suicide, 62
Summerhill, 144, 147-48, 163
Supreme Court, 36, 41, 45, 96, 121
Swaggert, Jimmy, 29
Sweden, 74
Switzerland, 74
Symonds, John Addington, 42

T

Taiwan, 74
Teacher Corps, 129
teacher education, 126-27
textbooks, 157
thalidomide, 35
Transportation Department, 24
Tsongas, Paul, 99
Tuskegee Normal and Industrial Institute, 121
TV commercials, 63, 94, 98-105, 107, 112, 142
TV debates, 105
TV evangelists, 29, 31, 133

U

U.S. Commission on Civil Rights, 24
U.S. Tobacco Company, 17
uninsured, 86, 90
uninsured pool, 73
Upward Bound, 129

V

Veterans Administration, 24
Videos, 142
Virginia, 62
Vista, 129
Vote Smart, 108-09
voucher system, 157-63

W

Wall Street, 25
Wallach, E. Bob, 24
Washington, Booker T., 120
Washington D.C., 58
Washington, D.C., 49
Washington Post, 100
Watergate, 16, 26
Watson, John B., 122
Watt, James G., 24
Wedtech, 24
Wells, H.G., 111
Whittle experiment, 162, 167